The Most Popular
Freak in School

The Most Popular Freak in School

By:

Crystal Tyler

Disclaimer
The Most Popular Freak in School by Crystal Tyler
Copyright 2019 –

CONTENTS

Once Upon a Time in a faraway kingdom, there lived a beautiful princess. Not just beautiful in appearance but also at heart. She wasn't like the other people in her kingdom. She was unique. But the kingdom didn't appreciate her, and she found very little kindness from others. Rather than receiving the smiles, compliments, and kind words that she would give those around her, the princess was often greeted with cold stares, insults, and laughter. Throughout the years the princess struggled with the rejection she faced. She felt alone and afraid of what her future would hold. While other princesses would find their Prince Charming and live out their happily ever after, this princess started to wonder if she would ever get to experience a happy ending. She dreamed of nothing more than a knight in shining armor to save her from her tower and for them to live out their happy ending. But as the years went on, the princess grew more independent, rebellious, and tough-skinned, and the sounds of peasants laughing at her got quieter. After enough self-pity, she developed a love for art and sewing and hoped that these hobbies could lead her to a different happy ending. She kept a strong exterior, for she had to deal with trials that other princesses didn't have to deal. This princess was trapped in prison like no other. She was forced to live in the body of a boy and go to high school.

CRYSTAL'S PHONE

September 14th
7:09 AM

Tracy: Ethan, doesn't your bus come soon? Get out of the bathroom!

Tracy: The fact that I have to text you because it's the only way to get your attention is sad.

Crystal: I'm heading out now, I'm just making sure I have everything.

Tracy: Don't you have a test first period today? I told you to go early!

Crystal: I'm leaving now.

Tracy: You better not be late!

Crystal: I won't.

Crystal: Have a nice day.

CRYSTAL'S DIARY
September 15th

     I have somehow completed my first week of junior year. I honestly thought I was gonna be dead meat by the end of freshman year, and I didn't even start wearing makeup until I was a sophomore. I remember right before freshman year started was such a stressful time. We all know about the legacy that High School has with its athletic department and their performing arts programs. Also, how the school colors, purple and white in my case, are forced to become everyone's favorite colors. Then there are the deans that'll interrupt whatever conversations you're having in the hallway as they yell "walk and talk".

     At the start of high school, I truly thought I had the potential to come off as a regular teenage boy, but I knew with my interests in makeup and dresses I had no hopes of being an average high school student. So, I fell into the nerd category. That is until I wore makeup for the first time one day. From then on, I lived among the freaks. And on the last day of sophomore year when I showed up to school in a purple wig, full face of intense makeup, and whatever girly but still edgy clothes I could

12

find, I rightfully earned my title, *The Most Popular Freak in School.*

Now that we've returned for our junior year the closest thing, I've received to a welcome from my classmates was shocked faces, a fear of making eye contact, and a sense of intimidation, and I live for every moment of it.

As proud as I am of my individuality, I would love to get to share my story with more people. I just wish there was a better beginning to tell.

My Story (as of now)

I was born on June 29th, 1999, in Staten Island, New York. I lived in a black and white Victorian house on the south shore in a close-knit neighborhood with my mom, my dad, and much, much older siblings from my dad's previous marriage. I never had any full siblings that had the same birth parents like me, or any kids around my age to spend time. I seemed to be my own generation in my family. All my siblings and cousins were 10+ years older than me. I was always one to stand out, but I often felt intimidated by everyone being so much bigger than me at an early age. It felt easier and easier to fade. As early as 3, I couldn't let go of the crayons and paper. I embraced my gift to create as soon as I could, and it lit up my world throughout the next decade of growing up in a broken home where it felt no one really wanted me around, and in a school where I was cast aside as the weird kid. Growing up in Staten Island isn't easy for queer kids. It takes the bravest souls to do it. I'm lucky enough to be one of them, among many others. My struggle with sexuality started at 12 when I had a crush on a boy at school, but once I embraced it and accepted myself, it was nothing but rainbows from there. I do identify as trans. I always identified more with girls. I believe my body should not determine the lifestyle I live. I started wearing makeup to school at 15, and all the insults, the bullying, the negativity, didn't exist. I was powerful; I was beautiful. I was me. Throughout my life, many important characters have come into play to shape me into the queen I am today. They all inspired the six main characters that brought to life the first play that I started writing when I was 15 and got put on stage 4 times when I was 18

Crystal is the name that I eventually adapted for my drag name, Crystal Tyler. Crystals catch the light and create a rainbow, and that's what inspired me. She's helped me come to terms with my own identity, exploring the beautiful and fascinating spectrum of LGBTQ identities. Crystal, born as Ethan, is a brave trans person whose pride in her identity is more important to her than the opinions of others. But of course, she's still human, and can't just shut out all of the negativity; she can only dial it down to a whisper.

Tracy is a woman Crystal's father knew from the bar. Tracy was around ever since Crystal was a baby. She became the only mother in her life. She was nice, but you could still sense a fakeness to her kindness. From a young age, Crystal knew she couldn't entirely trust her. But Tracy was a very wealthy woman from a rich family, and she was able to help Crystal's dad afford to keep the house after he lost his first wife. She's even paid for a majority of Crystal's college fund. So, Crystal decided to ignore it and except Tracy into the family, because by the time she started middle school, Tracy was officially her new stepmother.

Anna is Tracy's daughter and Crystal's stepsister. They started middle school together. At first, Crystal and Anna were close; they both dealt with the loss of parents at a young age and helped each other get through it. But as time went on, Anna got more pretty, more popular, and Crystal, the bullied kid, wasn't good enough for her anymore. By 8th grade, Anna cut ties with Crystal at school and barely talked to her at home. And since Tracy's love of wine seemed to take away from her abilities to keep house, all the housework usually fell on Crystal's lap.

Drew is Anna's jock boyfriend. He plays football or something like that. After Crystal's drag debut the last day of school the kids who I guess we'll call the bullies will only yell insults from down the hall or whisper them behind her back. But Drew's never afraid to try to pick a fight in front of a crowd. And she's never afraid to clap back. One of my favorite incidents was when he tried to take a video of her as she was going into the girl's bathroom, while all his jock friends could do was stand behind him and laugh as he screamed at her calling her a queer. And all Crystal said in

16

response, right to the camera was, "And so is that haircut."

Maria is Crystal's best friend. They met in middle school during tutoring; Maria said she thought the tutor was cute, and Crystal said, "I think so too." Maria went on to say that she liked girls too and Crystal told her that she feels like she is a girl. And from then on, it was them against the world. She's the one that first did Crystal's makeup and helped her get dressed on the last day of school. She's the one helping her get ready and finish my makeup in school when Crystal was either running late or didn't want Tracy to see her. She's the one who truly had her back.

Tom... we can save that later.

So, I hope it all comes out to a beautiful story. If not, it's still only the beginning.

CRYSTAL'S PHONE

September 21st
7:01 AM

Maria: Hey, I got to school early, text me when you're on your way.

Crystal: Hey! I'm heading out soon. Meet me by the bathrooms. I did my makeup; I just need to change.

Maria: Just wear your outfit under a hoodie and sweatpants, then run in the bathroom and take them off, then just stuff them in your bag.

Crystal: Smart! What about shoes? I wanted to wear heels today, but there's no way I'll be able to get away with wearing them as I leave.

Maria: Leave with flats, I'll grab the floral print heels you left at my house the other day.

Crystal: OMG, I forgot you had those, thank you so much!

Maria: No problem!

Crystal: I don't know if I'll make it in time for the 1st Period, but I'm supposed to have a substitute teacher for Chemistry today.

Maria: I'm fine with missing 1st, it's Gym, I just don't want to be late for Art 2nd period.

Crystal: It's fine we're supposed to have a sub in Art too.

Maria: Where are all our teachers going?

Crystal: Why is that something we want to question?

Maria: You're not wrong.

Crystal: I'll be there soon!

Maria: Alright, see you soon <3

CRYSTAL

<u>Act 1 Scene 2: School Hallway</u>

(Lights go on. A small crowd of teenagers is walking, chatting, and retrieving items from their lockers. Crystal, still presenting as a boy, is about to go into the girl's bathroom but stops. Drew approaches her.)

Drew: What's the matter (air quoting) "Crystal"? Don't know which one to use, huh?

Crystal: Well no, you see, I'm just patiently waiting for everyone to leave, so I don't grab too much attention. What about you, Drew, how are those four to five boyfriends you're always seen walking the halls with?

(Maria walks onto the stage and approaches Crystal from behind. Drew leaves defeated while the other students trail behind. Crystal and Maria are the only ones left on stage.)

Maria: (Sarcastically) Wow, Crystal! You really have a way with people.

Crystal: I do, don't I?

(They hug.)

Maria: How was your weekend?

Crystal: (sighs) As good as it'll ever be, having to deal with Tracy.

Maria: (rolling her eyes) Come on… your stepmom is so lovely. I don't understand why you always complain about her.

Crystal: Try living with her for most of your 16 years then talk to me. Now I got to get dressed, be my lookout.

Maria: But we're already late to art.

Crystal: Don't worry; we're supposed to have a sub. I'm just hoping everyone stays in class; I don't want anyone trying to give me a problem this early.

Maria: Don't worry, I got your back!

Crystal: (smiling) Wow, was I wise to choose you for my best friend.

(They hug again, leaving the stage. The lights dim.)

CRYSTAL'S DIARY

September 21st

So today I met someone that made me feel almost every emotion ever, from annoyed, too excited, too nervous. Maria's other best friend, or cousin, whatever he is, Tom. I've known who Tom was for a while. He was always just another jock, so I knew to avoid him because I assumed that I already knew exactly what he thought of me. But today I found out I was wrong. I didn't know his opinion of me at all, and I certainly did not have the right idea about him.

I met him in art today. Tom had just gotten transferred to our class, and when he came up to Maria all excited about sharing a class with her, she introduced us. He gave me one of the firmest handshakes and kindest smiles I've ever received. But I didn't think much of it, as I was sure he gave that same charming smile to everyone. I admit it's a good time looking at him. He has dark hair, dark eyes, a muscular figure, and a very handsome face. I had also recognized him from the drama club.

Today when I met Maria outside of school after last period Tom was with her. Drew came out and pulled him to the side.

"What are you doing with that freak? Are you friends with him?" I heard Drew say. Immediately Tom responded, "As a matter of fact, she is my friend." As touched as I was to hear Tom say this, Drew continued to belittle me saying, "Why would you be friends with someone like that?"

I tried to stand up for myself, and Drew stood right back. Even when he tried to act tough, I could tell there was something cowardly about him. After he walked off, I almost went after him, but Maria pulled me back.

Before she left, she looked at me and said, "Don't let it bother you. I have to go." We hugged, she left for the train station, and I started walking down to the bus stop; still a little shook up after what had just happened. I was in a mood to just be left alone, but I'd soon come to realize I wasn't.

"Hey" I heard a voice from behind me say as I was walking. I turned around to see Tom running up next to me.

"Are you okay?" he asked. As much as I wanted to believe a cute football player was trying to be nice to me, there's no way I was gonna fall for that Prince Charming act. "What do you want?" I replied. "Well, after what just happened, I wanted to make sure you were okay," he said. The conversation continued, and I kept trying to push him away. But he didn't leave.

"Why do you seem to have such an interest in me?" I said as I started to walk away again. "Why is it you have such a wall up?" said Tom. Realizing this kid wasn't gonna leave me alone, I decided to give him the satisfaction of helping me. "I just wish I could be myself without others having something nasty to say about it, to my face or behind my back. That's all," I replied. "You don't have to convince people you're tough as nails to get by. Do you have any idea how strong it is to come out as trans in high school and be as open as you are about it?" he said. I was still waiting for some indication, some sign that he wasn't for real, but it wouldn't come. It all felt genuine. By this point, we were standing right by the bus stop, and from down the street, I saw my bus turn the corner and start driving down toward us. At that point, he said he had to go. "It was nice talking to you!" was the last thing he said before running off.

I got on the bus and spent the entire bus ride in the clouds, until the bus let me off, and I started walking down the block to my house. Now I'm here, in my room, writing it all down to further convince myself that it was real.

God, I hope it was...

Tom

The First Piece of Inspiration

Tom is the character that embodied everything my ideal Prince Charming had, from good looks to a perfect personality. He is the first character that inspired the overall story. Two people I knew from high school served as the inspiration for him. The first is the boy from the bus stop. I met him when I was a freshman in high school. I first saw him when I went to see a school play the beginning of that year, and I thought he was cute but thought nothing of it after that. I eventually saw him again in the drama club, and I realized he was friends with my best friend at the time. I told him I thought he did good in the play I saw him in, and he reacted with a shrug that came off as "Yeah, I know." He was a little bit of a dick at the time, which only made him even more attractive to me. In fact, my best friend that I had met him through already had a crush on him.

Besides drama club, my friends and I would go to the video game club, which was like an afternoon hang out in the teachers' lounge Fridays after school. He would be there, and I'd be with my friends on the other side of the room, but I'd be looking at him most of the time. I felt my walls go up, but not all the way. Our friendship did continue, and before I knew it, by the end of my freshman year, I was head over heels for him, blinded by a high school crush.

On a bus ride home, some of my friends teased me over my crush. Some boys from the back of the bus overheard, and apparently, a lot was said about me when I got off the bus. The next day I caught him the hallway and told him it was a joke.

I tried to get over it that summer but seeing him again the next year didn't help that at all. I saw him again in drama club, and in video game club. This was when we started taking the bus home together. Often, I would stay on the bus and walk with him, because I just couldn't get enough of him. At that point, I couldn't tell what I liked so much anymore. These strong feelings started to unravel, and eventually, so did the rest of me.

The point when this crush changed my life was when I felt like I could trust him enough to be the first person I give my truth to. For the first time in my life, I said out loud to someone, "I am trans." That broke the ice for me. I came back from Thanksgiving weekend, ready for the first drama club meeting for the month of December. I was cutting class with a friend. She was doing her makeup, and I said I wanted to wear some too. All I had in my bag was a red lipstick from my collection of Halloween makeup, and she helped me put it on. I went to a drama club meeting that day, getting only praise, even from him. On the bus ride home that day, he spoke, laughing, about how he admired my outgoingness. But I was still taken back, still human, yet insecure. He told me something that stays with me forever and served inspiration for this play and this story. *Use Your Disadvantages to Your Advantage.*

CRYSTAL MEETS TOM

Act 1 Scene 3: Art Class

(Lights go on. The students have art supplies on their desks, while a substitute teacher sits at the instructor's, filling out the attendance sheet.)

Maria: (Entering) Come on, Crystal!

(Crystal enters in feminine black clothes and makeup.)

Substitute: Girls, you're late.

Crystal: (To Maria) Of course when we're late there's a sub that actually cares if you're late.

Substitute: Names, please.

Maria: I'm Maria.

Crystal: Crystal (Pointing to the attendance sheet), but on there, it says Ethan.

Substitute: I'm sorry… I'm confused.

Crystal: Okay, I'll spell it out real slow for you. My birth certificate says male, but I feel more at peace as female. Try taking a cultural competency class.

(They move away from the substitute. Tom approaches them.)

Tom (Smiling with wide eyes): Maria, hey! I didn't know you were in this class.

Maria: Oh my god, hi! (Hugs Tom) Did you get transferred?

Tom: Yeah, for like the fifth time this year.

Maria: (Looking at his schedule) We have lunch together too!

Crystal: Uh, Maria, who's that?

Maria: Yay, you two can finally meet! Crystal this is my cousin, Tom, Tom this is Crystal…

Tom: (Shaking Crystal's hand) It's nice to meet you finally. I've heard a lot about you.

Crystal: Really? Like what?

Tom: Just that you're pretty, friendly, funny, creative, sarcastic.

Crystal: (To Tom) Well, I don't like to brag. (To Maria) Can we talk real quick?

Maria: Sure (The girls move over.) What's up?

Crystal: Why did you tell him so much about me?

Maria: When he started coming here, he asked about my friends at school, so I mentioned you. God…

Crystal: Does he happen to know everything about me?

Maria: Maybe he does.

Crystal: Great.

Maria: He's not like that, don't put up a wall around him, he's a nice guy. If he were a jerk, he would've said something mean by now, and I would've slapped him for it.

Crystal: Okay...

Maria: Good (pushing Crystal towards Tom). Now go make friends with him!

(They walk back over to Tom.)

Crystal: So, is this your first time in an art class?

Tom: No, (showing Crystal his sketchbook) I've been taking it since sophomore year.

Crystal: (Surprised) Wow, you're really good.

Tom: Thanks. What about you?

Crystal: (Showing Tom her sketchbook) I've been drawing since I was five.

Tom: (Impressed) You're really good too!

Crystal: Thank you. So besides art, what else are you into?

Tom: I did football for a while.

Maria: (Laughing) This should be good...

Crystal: So I'm guessing you know Drew and all those (air quoting) "lovely" individuals?

Tom: Yeah, you're friends with them?

Crystal: (Turning a little red) Not really. No.

Tom: Yeah, I know they're not the nicest people around. Drew quit football or got kicked off. We'll never really know, but seriously, don't worry; I'm not a jerk like them.

Crystal: (Under her breathe) That's what they all say.

(Maria nudges her. The bell rings.)

Crystal: Damn, how late were we?

Maria: You're the one that took 15 minutes doing her makeup. (To Tom) What do you have now?

Tom: Math. I basically got a whole new schedule.

(They enter the hallway into a crowd of kids. The school's mean girl, Anna, walks out…)

Anna: Out of my way everyone, I have a class to get to!

Crystal: (To Maria) Oh look, it's Satan in a skirt.

Maria: Please, don't be rude.

Tom: (Looking at Anna) Who is that?

Crystal: Her name's Anna; the schools #2 diva.

Tom: Who is #1?

Crystal: (Laughing) Me.

Anna: (To Crystal) Who the hell are you looking at?

Crystal: No one of any relevance.

Anna: (Attempting to walk away) Why don't you go look for clothes that fit you properly?

Crystal: Gladly. Why don't you go do the same?

(Anna stops for a second, turns around and looks at her, then exits.)

Tom: How do you know her?

Crystal: (Looking away) Just do, I guess. I'm going to class. See you guys later.

(The crowd leaves the stage. Lights dim)

Act 1 Scene 4: Outside School

(Lights are on. There is a bench and a bus stop. Maria and Tom walk to the bench where Crystal's waiting.)

Crystal: Maria, can I come over? I don't want to go home yet.

(Tom looks at Crystal and Maria as if he needs to get a word in.)

Maria: (To Crystal) Sorry, I have a doctor's appointment today.

(Drew comes out, sees Tom and pulls him aside.)

Drew: Tom, why are you talking to that freak? Are you friends with him?

Tom: (Looking at Crystal) As a matter of fact (emphasizing) she is my friend.

Drew: Why would you make friends with someone like that?

Tom: What do you mean "someone like that"? I know she's not exactly like us, but she's still a human being.

Drew: (To Tom) Look, just be careful, you don't know his intentions.

Crystal: (Overhearing) Are you two seriously talking about me, right in front of me?

Drew: Why don't you take your frilly dresses, heels, and makeup and get out of my face!? (Beginning to walk off)

Crystal: (Trying to follow him) Oh yeah? Well, these heels are bigger than your (Maria quickly covers her mouth as Drew exits.)

Maria: Are you okay?

Crystal: I'll be fine.

Maria: (Putting her hands on Crystal's shoulders) Listen, don't let it bother you. I got to go; I love you.

(They hug, and Maria leaves. Crystal sits down on the bench, and Tom approaches her.)

Tom: Hey

Crystal: What do you want?

Tom: You seem upset, are you okay?

Crystal: What, you're not laughing it up with your buddy, Drew?

Tom: Drew is not my buddy, he's a jerk, I only tolerated him when we were on the football team together, and now he still thinks we're friends. Maria's always told me you never care what people say or think about you. What makes Drew any different?

Crystal: (Getting up from the bench, trying to walk away) Can you just leave me alone?

Tom: (Following her) I'm just trying to help.

Crystal: (Turns around, facing him) Why is it you have such an interest in me?

Tom: Why is it you have such a wall up?

Crystal: You're lucky that you're my best friend's cousin.

Tom: What's wrong?

Crystal: Of course, I care what others say or think about me. It just sucks that I can't be myself… (Pause) without someone having something to say about it.

Tom: You don't have to convince people that you're tough as nails to get by.

Crystal: I don't want people thinking I'm weak.

Tom: Everyone has insecurities, and it does not make them weak. Do you have any idea how strong it is to come out as trans in high school and be as open as you are about it?

(Crystal looks away.)

Tom: Besides, people like Drew won't matter after high school. You'll never see him again unless he's at the drive-thru window handing you your burger and fries.

Crystal: (Making eye contact, laughing) Thank you.

Tom: How did you get the courage to come out?

Crystal: It was painstaking. But someone once said to me, use your disadvantages to your advantage. My disadvantage was gender dysphoria, so I made it into something beautiful.

Tom: (Smiling and looking at his watch) I got to go. It was nice talking to you!

Crystal: You too.

(Tom exits, following Crystal. The Lights dim.)

CRYSTAL'S PHONE

September 21st

5:03 PM

Crystal: Hey, it's Crystal.

Tom: Hey! How are you?

Crystal: I'm good thanks! I wanted to say thank you for earlier.

Tom: Of course!
Tom: To be honest, I never thought you would be bothered by someone else's opinion. I was always impressed with the way you presented yourself; it takes so much courage to do what you do, especially in such a conservative environment like this

Crystal: Aw, that means a lot, thank you so much! I try to come off as confident as I can, but I'm still human.
Crystal: I always thought the island was conservative too, but I never thought a jock would agree.

Tom: Are you kidding? Mostly everyone talks about the same things and has the same exact opinions, most of those opinions being very closed minded. It's amazing, there are people like you to challenge those opinions.

Tom: I also can't stand how, as an athlete, I'm basically required to wear purple and white every day. There are so many other colors in the rainbow!

Crystal: The overkill with purple is actually one thing I don't mind. It's one of my favorite colors.
Crystal: Pink and blue create purple, so it's like combining femininity and masculinity to create something new. Purple represents gender neutrality.

Tom: Oh, wow, I never knew that.

Crystal: The one thing I don't like the most about our school is how favoritive everything is. Unless you're talented or good looking it's like you don't matter and you're just cast to the side.
Crystal: Then again, I can't complain, I'd rather be the underdog anyway.

Tom: You're better off; you probably have a lot more freedom.

Crystal: I never thought being popular came with so many hardships.

Tom: It's almost always expected of me to act a certain way. When I try to be myself, people seem to not understand it.

Crystal: I'm not gonna lie, I will admit I had a certain idea of you before Maria introduced us, with all I've put

up with from the jocks, especially Drew, I feel safer
keeping my guard up.
Crystal: But really, you've changed my perspective of
a lot. You're the first guy, let alone jock, that has shown
me respect in a long time.

Tom: I'm happy to show you you're worthy of respect
as everyone else.

Crystal: That means a lot thank you.

Tom: You're welcome.
Tom: So, if it's okay to ask, how exactly do you
identify?
Tom: Sorry, maybe that was too personal. What
pronouns do you prefer?

Crystal: No, it's okay! It's important to be open about
it so others know how to respect it. I identify as trans,
more specifically, a demigirl or transfeminine. I float on
the feminine side of the gender spectrum. I prefer
female pronouns.
Crystal: I just believe manhood and womanhood are
lifestyles that your body shouldn't have to choose for
you. And if you have qualities of both, that's even
better.

Tom: May I confess something?

Crystal: Sure.

Tom: I feel that way when it comes to sexual orientation. There shouldn't have to be countless labels and definitions to put on love. With the gender spectrum being so diverse, a partner should be chosen based on who they are. I'm just completely blind to their body, and whatever they identify as I'll know to respect.

Crystal: Are you trying to come out to me as pansexual?

Tom: Yeah, I guess.

Crystal: Oh, wow.
Crystal: Does anyone else know?

Tom: I don't talk about it a lot. It's not really anyone else's business.
Tom: I just don't wanna deal with or hear the backlash for that because I know it'll be a lot.

Crystal: You need to meet your people and get to know more about the LGBTQ community.
Crystal: You should come to GSA!

Tom: GSA?

Crystal: The Gay-Straight Alliance! It's not that big, but you'll get to meet other queer students. You might make a friend or two. It meets on Thursdays after school, in the same room where the Comic Book Club meets.

Tom: I don't think I'm doing anything Thursday.

Crystal: Cool!

Crystal: So, the actual first meeting isn't until October 15th, but Maria and I are helping plan for the year with the president and other head members. But anyone else is welcome.

Tom: Okay, I'll try to go!

Crystal: Awesome!

ANNA'S PHONE

September 21st

1: 33 PM

Drew: Hey Baby!
Drew: Why weren't you in school today??

Anna: I was, I got my attendance taken and left.
Anna: It's not like Tracy would have anything to say,
she'll be asleep long past I'm supposed to be home
anyway.

Drew: How is it you and Ethan come from the same
household, yet he's in school every day until the last bell
at 2:30?

Anna: How is it any of your business?
Anna: Besides, he doesn't even go to every class; he
skips the first and last period all the time.

Drew: Something happened with him this morning.

Anna: Oh?

Drew: Right before the first period when everyone
was getting to class, I walked past him by the
bathrooms. I was with the boys, so I yelled out, "Hey
Crystal, don't know which one to use?"

Drew: Then, as we're laughing, I hear him say, "I'm just waiting for my friend, how are all your boyfriends doing."

Drew: I swear if the deans weren't walking the halls, I would've knocked him out.

Anna: I'm sure you would've taught him a real good lesson, tough guy.

Drew: It's not funny!
Drew: You need to get him under control

Anna: Because you want to start problems with him, I need to "keep him under control"? Why don't you grow up? We're not in middle school anymore.

Drew: Oh, like you're so mature?

Anna: You don't know what it's been like living with him. What he does is unnatural! It's scary having that in your own house.

Drew: I know baby, I'm sorry.
Drew: You wanna come over?

Anna: Sure, piss me off and invite me over.
Anna: Smooth.

Drew: You're right, I'm sorry.
Drew: Still wanna come over??

Drew: Baby???

8:08 PM

Drew: Hey
Drew: Babe??

Anna: What's up?

Drew: Have you seen Ethan at all today?

Anna: No, I went out as soon as he got home. Why?

Drew: He tried to piss me off again after school.

Anna: He tried to, or he did?

Drew: He tried to get nasty for no reason.

Anna: No reason at all?

Drew: He was with Tom. I just wanted to be sure
Ethan wasn't trying to creep on him.

Anna: What? You're joking. Why were they with each
other?

Drew: I don't know.

Anna: Why would he want anything to do with Ethan?

Drew: I don't know babe, but it's not something you should worry about.

Anna: Oh, but you should?

Drew: Tom is my friend; I'm just trying to look out for him.

Anna: It's just very strange to me.

Drew: Yeah, but Tom's no fool, it was probably a one-time thing.
Drew: Babe? You there??

Anna: I just need to see this for myself.
Anna: I guess I'll see you at school this week.

Drew: Awesome, at least there's something to look forward to now.
Drew: So, how was your day?

Anna: I'm tired, good night.

ANNA'S DIARY

September 22nd

So, it seems Ethan has taken a liking to Tom, Drew's friend that I've had a crush on since middle school. Even though we were never close or anything, we always knew each other, and I guess I just always admired him from afar. He's just so hot and has such a kind and open personality. No one can really blame me for dating Drew so I get closer to him. But we still haven't connected like the way I want. It's still just a Hi and Bye kind of thing.

Drew texted me to say Ethan somehow has sparked a friendship with him, something I try everything in my power to do, but now Ethan is somehow friends with him out of nowhere? It was hard to believe at first, so, for once I stayed the whole day at school, and between classes, in the halls, I saw Tom talking with Ethan, walking with him, and laughing with him.

I remember just watching from down the hall as Tom and Ethan were acting like the best of friends, and I can't even get anything out of Tom past a half-assed "Hi."

The last thing Ethan is going to take away from me is the boy I've had feelings bottled up for since 8th grade. And that's a promise.

Act 1 Scene 5: School Hallway

(The next day, there is chatter in the halls, lockers are open, and students are storing and retrieving books. Crystal stands in front of hers, staring out into space. Maria approaches her.)

Maria: I'm bugging out. With my doctor's appointment yesterday, I had no time to study for this math test, and I (Snapping her fingers) Crystal…. Crystal!

Crystal: (Coming to) Yeah Tom… I mean Maria.

Maria: What is with you today?

Crystal: Nothing, just tired, I guess.

Maria: Are we still going to GSA today?

Crystal: Yeah.

Maria: Oh and Tom said you invited him to come…

Crystal: Yeah. Why, has he talked about me at all?

Maria: No, why?

Crystal: No reason, I guess.

Maria: You were looking at him all weird in art today (Reading Crystal) it's like you….

Crystal: What?

Maria: You like him.

Crystal: No, I don't.

Maria: Yeah, you do.

Crystal: No, I don't.

Maria: Yeah, you do.

Crystal: (Eying Maria) Okay, maybe I do.

Maria: (Gasping) Crystal (Hugging her) …this is so cute!

(Maria releases Crystal.)

Maria: Wait. So, you do like my cousin? Ew, why?

Crystal: Yesterday, I just saw a sweet, compassionate side to him. He helped me feel better after what happened with Drew. Plus, he's really cute.

Maria: Aw, that's so beautifully corny…

Crystal: Yesterday, he admitted to me that he's not exactly straight either.

Maria: That surprises you? I knew that kid was gay since I was eight.

Crystal: Whatever. I know not to fall for a guy the moment I see him.

(Tom approaches Crystal and Maria from behind.)

Tom: Hey, guys.

(Crystal trips.)

Maria: (Walking off) I'm going to give you guys some privacy. (Running off.)

Crystal: No, Maria, come back, wait! (To Tom) Hi.

Tom: Hey Crystal! I'm excited for GSA.

Crystal: You're so pretty.

Tom: What?

Crystal: Nothing.

(Crystal and Tom laugh awkwardly)

Maria: (Enters) You're doing great!

Crystal: (To Maria) Shut Up! (To Tom) I'm sorry. I'm just not feeling good right now.

Tom: Oh, okay, well, I'll see you later!

Crystal: You too! (Giggling and putting her head down.)

(Tom exits. Maria sprints to Crystal.)

Maria: If you want my honest opinion, that went really well.

(Crystal's head is still down, giving Maria the finger. Lights dim.)

CRYSTAL'S PHONE

September 23rd

6: 31 PM

Jackie: Hey Crystal! It's Jackie, this year's GSA president, I just want to make sure you're definitely coming tomorrow!

Crystal: Hey, I know it's you, I saved your number after you got elected at the end of last year. And yes, I'm definitely coming, and of course, I'll be with Maria.

Jackie: Cool!

Crystal: We were also gonna bring another friend with us if that's okay.

Jackie: Of course! Anyone's welcome, and I can use all the help I can get before the first official meeting next month. What's their name?

Crystal: Tom, he's a close family friend of Marias. He's a junior.

Jackie: Is he on the football team?

Crystal: Yeah.

Jackie: Wow, a football player has never set foot in GSA before.

Crystal: I know, crazy right? He's a really nice guy.

Jackie: I'll take your word for it!

Crystal: As long as we're talking, can I ask you something?

Jackie: Sure!

Crystal: I've always wanted to run for GSA president ever since freshman year. Even though I was eligible last year to run, I wasn't confident enough. Besides, everyone said you were gonna get it. Do you have any advice for if I decide to run for next year?

Jackie: Since I'll be graduating this June, you'll definitely be eligible to be president next year! You have to be likable and easy to talk to. You'll have a lot of responsibilities, from coming up with ideas for meetings to being a role model for the younger kids. It's a lot, but it's not difficult if you stay on top of things, and it's very rewarding in the end.

Crystal: Thank you so much. It means a lot! I hope I have what it takes.

Jackie: The first step is to tell yourself that you do. I believe in you.

Crystal: Thanks so much!

Jackie: Anytime. See you tomorrow!

September 24th

4:51 PM

Jackie: Welcome to this year's GSA group chat everyone!

Maria: Hello all.

Gus: Okay, but the first order of business. Can we please get more than one box of doughnuts for next week?

Suzy: I'm sure that's not the first thing we need to worry about Gus.

Luke: Yeah, our main concern should obviously be what flavor of doughnuts we're gonna get for next week.

Maria: We need more chocolate.

Jackie: Relax, I'll make sure everyone gets enough doughnuts next week. As you all know, the first official meeting is October 15th. We have to start spreading the word now. I'm thinking we all design fliers and start hanging them up by next week?

Luke: Should the fliers all have a similar theme?

Gus: Rainbows, duh.

Jackie: The theme for the fliers should be equality. They should all say the same thing, Gay Straight Alliance, meets every Thursday in Room D202, starting October 15th, and it's always best to say things like "Bring Friends" and "Everyone's Welcome." Besides that, you can get creative. Just make sure it's school appropriate.

Suzy: I started drawing out drafts on my way home! I'll send pics later.

Luke: Crystal? You there?

Crystal: Hi.

Suzy: What's up with you? You're never this quiet in group chats.

Gus: Real question, why did you bring that jock today?

Luke: He didn't even really talk much.

Crystal: It was his first time coming, he's just starting to get to know the club.

Gus: But why would you bring a straight boy to GSA?

Crystal: Why not? Isn't this club about including everyone?

Jackie: Crystal's right, GSA accepts anyone. Besides, I could use extra help in getting ready for the first meeting.

Gus: But from a jock? They hate us more than anyone else in the school.

Crystal: Hates us? He doesn't even know us. He came today and is gonna continue coming to meetings. How do you expect to be accepted if you're gonna be this closed minded toward someone else?

Gus: Why are you all of a sudden standing up for a jock when you were talking bad about Drew and his friends less than a week ago?

Crystal: I'm gonna go work on my drafts for the flier, I'll talk to you guys later.

Maria: Gus, Tom is a close family friend of mine, he's basically my cousin. He wouldn't do or say anything mean to us or behind our backs. He knows I'd kill him if he did.

Gus: Whatever, but if he gets added to this group chat, I'm suing...

Suzy: Suing who?

Luke: The "walk and talk" guy.

Gus: I wish! When I'm in a heated conversation over getting a one on homework, a man yelling "walk and talk" in my ear is not what I need.

Suzy: Stop, he's really supportive of us and GSA!

Gus: You're right, I'll sue the chorus teacher that always wears a plastic crown

Jackie: I hope you guys are designing your fliers!

Maria: We're doing our best.

Suzy: I am!

Jackie: Oh, as long as we're talking, later this year there's gonna be a masquerade ball for high school GSAs across the city. I found out about it at the Pride Center. I don't know all the details, but I'll keep you all updated!

October 14th

2:44 PM

Jackie: Hey guys! Who's excited for tomorrow?

Suzy: I am!

Gus: I think Jackie's more excited than anyone.

Maria: Wouldn't you be excited if you were president? She only gets it for one year; she should be excited!

Jackie: Thanks, Maria!

Maria: Of course! I'm so excited for you, your speech when you were running last year was so good, I can't wait to see what you do this year.

Luke: Are you nervous?

Jackie: Aw, thank you, Maria! There's definitely a lot of nerves that come with it, but I know I'll realize tomorrow how much it's worth it.
Jackie: My main objective is to be able to offer a safe place to the younger kids. I know how hard it is being queer in high school. I can't imagine how intimidating it is for younger students. They deserve to have a safe place and know that there is support.

Suzy: That is so beautiful! Crystal's always said the same thing.
Suzy: OMG, what if she runs for next year?

Gus: Crystal for president? Shouldn't the president of such a loving club not suffer severe resting bitch face?

Maria: Oh, because you'd do a better job?

Jackie: Enough arguing, I wanna go over who's bringing what tomorrow.

Suzy: I'll make cupcakes, and I think Luke was gonna get plates and napkins.

Luke: I am.
Luke: Also, why is Crystal inactive again?

Gus: She's probably daydreaming over her new football player friend.

Luke: New? They've practically been skipping down the halls together every day for almost a month now.
Luke: Maria, tell me, even now, they're not a thing.

Maria: I love how you talk about Crystal as if she's not even gonna see this.
Maria: And no, they're not a thing, they're calling each other friends for now.

Crystal added Tom to the chat

Luke: …….

Suzy: Hi Tom!

Gus: Crystal??
Gus: Whomst is this?

Crystal: What do you mean Whomst? It's Tom, the one who's been coming to meetings and helping Jackie.

Gus: Helping? He barely talks, whenever he does, it's to you.

Tom: Hi to you too, bud.

Luke: Hi cutie!

Gus: Look, I'm just trying to understand why a jock would want to be a part of a GSA.

Crystal: This club isn't just for queer students Gus, we welcome everyone of any sexuality and gender.

Maria: Preach!

Gus: He doesn't belong in the GSA. End of story.

Tom left the chat

Gus: Thank you!!

Crystal left the chat

Maria: That was way over the top, they did not deserve that.

Jackie: If anyone even goes off topic about GSA once you're getting removed from the chat.

Jackie: And they're owed an apology.

Suzy: Should I make the cupcakes rainbow or not?

October 14th

3:15 PM

Tom: I told you it was a bad idea to put me in that chat.

Crystal: I wanted you to be more involved and feel more comfortable sharing your ideas with them.

Tom: They don't like me. I care about the club, but maybe it's just not for me after all.

Crystal: Don't say that. There's supposed to be a lot of people coming tomorrow; you don't have to stand out if you don't want to. Besides, you've been a big help with the fliers and bulletin board. Jackie seems to think so too.

Tom: I do wanna come.

Crystal: Then come! Gus's opinions don't matter. He's as closed minded as everyone else.

Tom: Yeah, you're right.
Tom: No matter what anyone says, I'm so thankful for this friendship. I've learned so much from you.

Crystal: I agree. You make it easy to trust you.

Tom added Maria to the chat

Crystal: Until now.

Maria: Hi!! Sorry, I'm actually at Tom's, and I stole his phone to add myself.

Crystal: For what reason?

Maria: I needed to ask you something, but you were too busy texting Tom to answer me.

Crystal: Okay, what?

Maria: Where do I bring the drinks for the meeting tomorrow?

Crystal: Give it to the teacher in D202, he has a mini-fridge in his room.

Maria: You mean the teacher with the man bun?

Crystal: Yes Maria, the teacher with the man bun.

Maria: Got it.
Maria: Also, Suzy put in a word for you that you should be president next year.

Tom: Crystal, you'd make such a good president, you should go for it!

Crystal: Thank you guys, I do want to run for it this year.

Tom: Then run for it!

Crystal: I will.
Crystal: If you come tomorrow.

Tom: I will.

Crystal: Promise?

Tom: Promise.

GAY STRAIGHT ALLIANCE

Spreading the Message of Love,
Acceptance, & Equality

Meets Every Thursday in Room D202

Starting October 15th

Bring Friends

All Are Welcome

TOM'S NOTEBOOK

November 6th

Dear Crystal,

Yesterday was my 4th GSA meeting, and I can't be any more grateful for you introducing it to me. I never knew what inspiring people I was going to school with. A lot of people who go through the same feelings and emotions that I do. I never realized others would be dealing with the struggle of coming out, whether it's to family or friends, or in my case, both. I know it seems odd that I say I love it so much when I'm also the least talkative one in the room. But I've always believed someone can still enjoy something without being vocal about it. I'm so thankful that you helped me talk to Jackie about my ideas for the coming out meeting. Truthfully, it was the meeting I was looking forward to the most because it's the one I needed the most.

Jackie put people in pairs to talk about their coming out experiences and to answer any questions. And sure enough, I ended up with Gus. He seemed a bit bitter at first, but he told me about his coming out experience, and about the backlash, he's faced because of it. I asked him if I could trust him, and he responded with "I knew it!" but I brushed it off and told him I was pansexual, and I was seeking help regarding coming out. He smiled and said to me, "Once you accept yourself, you'll find how easy it is for everyone else to accept you." If it wasn't for you, I would've never gotten that opportunity.

GSA'S AND LGBTQ YOUTH
ARE
CORDIALLY INVITED TO
THE PRIDE CENTER'S
6TH ANNUAL MASQUERADE
BALL
HELD FRIDAY, MARCH 25TH,
AT 7:30 PM
AT THE PRIDE CENTER
$10 ADMISSION
BRING FRIENDS, ALL ARE
WELCOME AND ACCEPTED

Act 1 Scene 7: Bus Stop

(Lights go on. Crystal is waiting for Maria. Maria enters chatting with Tom.)

Tom: (To Maria) I have to go home.

Maria: (Dragging Tom) Your homework can wait. We need to see Crystal.

Tom: Uh, why?

Maria: Don't question me. (They walk over to Crystal.) Hey!

Crystal: (To Maria) There you are (Sees Tom and becomes flustered) Oh, hey Tom.

Tom: (Waving) Hey Crystal.

Maria: So I'm going to go over there (Pointing). You two can chat (walks to the side and watches over them.)

Tom: What's up with her?

Crystal: No clue. (Tries avoiding eye contact.)

Tom: So are you going to the masquerade dance?

Crystal: No, school dances are dumb, plus I don't have enough money

Tom: It's like $10.

Crystal: I don't have a good relationship with money. Are you going?

Tom: Maria's trying to make me go; she said to ask if you were going

Crystal: Did she now? Give me a sec. (Goes over to Maria.)

Maria: Did he ask you out yet?

Crystal: Don't think I don't know what you're doing.

Maria: What am I doing?

Crystal: You're trying to get Tom to ask me to that stupid masquerade dance.

Maria: (Turns away from Crystal and crosses her arms) How dare you accuse me of something like that?

Crystal: (Crosses her arms too) Are you denying it?

Maria: (Turns back around to face Crystal, unfolding her arms) Nope, that's totally my motive.

Crystal: Look, I can take care of myself.

Maria: (To Crystal) But you two are meant to be together and live happily ever after.

(Anna walks out, and bumps into Crystal.)

Crystal: Hey, watch it! What, did you get mascara in your eye?

Anna: Oh, I'm sorry, little miss attitude problem...

Crystal: Oh, shut your mouth...

Maria: (To Crystal) Ignore her, think about the masquerade party.

Anna: (Laughing) Crystal, who would be your date, let alone dance with you? No one wants a "girl" like you.

Tom: (Runs over) Hey, leave her alone, (Pointing to Crystal) she's just as much a girl as you are. Besides, she never did anything to you.

Anna: Whatever. I don't need to hear this, take your freak show somewhere else. (Exits)

Tom: You okay?

Crystal: I'll live.

Tom: (Leaving in a hurry, turning to Crystal) What she said wasn't true, if you go to this dance, I'll go, and I'll be more than happy to dance with you. (Exits)

Maria: (To Crystal) Still don't want to go?

Crystal: I'll talk to my stepmom.

(They smile and walk off; the lights dim.)

TRACY'S PHONE

November 10th

10:12 AM

Ethan: Hey, Tracy, I had to ask you something.

> Tracy: Shouldn't you be in class?

Ethan: It's my free period.

> Tracy: Well, at least you're not cutting like your dumbass sister.
> Tracy: You know you left the kitchen a mess this morning before you left.

Ethan: It looked pretty spotless to me.

> Tracy: Was the bowl in the sink yours?

Ethan: Could it have been yours, and you just forgot?

> Tracy: What do you want?

Ethan: I need to pay for a field trip next month, it's $20. I have some; maybe you can meet me half way?

> Tracy: You don't have $20?

Ethan: I don't really have time for a job since I have school and I'm basically working as a maid at the house full time. Remember?

Tracy: What's the field trip?

Ethan: A museum in the city, for art.

Tracy: When is it?

Ethan: March 25th, it's a Friday. I'll probably sleep over Maria's or something that night.

Tracy: I'll give you $10 when you get home.

Ethan: Thank you so much!

Tracy: Know every time you take my money, it comes out of your college fund.

Ethan: Got it. I'm sure it'll be worth it.
Ethan: Thanks again!

ANNA'S PHONE

November 19th

12:08 PM

Drew: Hey baby, are you in school?

Anna: Not now, I left after the 3rd period, I'm by the train station.

Drew: Alright, I just left so maybe I'll meet you?

Anna: Not now, I just wanna be alone today.

Drew: You wanna be alone every day lately.

Anna: I'm sorry, I just have a lot going on at home, and I haven't been feeling great.

Drew: What's going on? You know you can always talk to me if you need to.

Anna: I don't wanna bother you with it.

Drew: Is it your mom? You can't take what she says seriously.

Anna: I'm scared I'm gonna turn out like her.

Drew: You're stronger than she is.

Anna: I don't know...

Drew: Is there anything else stressing or upsetting you?

Anna: No...

Drew: It's Ethan, isn't it? What'd he do now?

Anna: I don't wanna talk about it.

Drew: I swear I'll get him; I'll go to that club he goes to and confront him.

Anna: You're all bark, no bite, and you know it.

Drew: I heard some of the other weirdos he hangs out with, like Maria and Gus, in the cafeteria today. They said something about a masquerade ball in the city. I swear I heard Maria say something about Ethan and Tom going together.
Drew: Babe??

Anna: You need to go to GSA today and find out what that's about.

Drew: If it'll make you happy.

Anna: It will.
Anna: I'm just concerned about Tom.

Anna: I'll see you tomorrow?

Drew: For sure.

CRYSTAL'S DIARY

November 19th

GSA is supposed to be a safe place for queer students. That's what Jackie's promise has been since before the first meeting. But the idea of it being safe becomes questionable when you see a security guard sitting outside the room. Going back to when I was a freshman, I remember there would always be a security guard sitting outside the room as we walked in for the meeting, during the meeting and would still be there when we left. We never talked about it, but we all knew what they were there for.

Today, as I was headed into my safe place with good friends, Anna's boy-toy, Drew made a guest appearance. I looked over my shoulder to see him approach Tom and ask to talk to him. I felt myself fuming, thinking about what awful things he had to say about me this time, but Maria quickly pushed me into the room. I made sure to stay close to the door, which was still open a crack, and you could barely hear Tom and Drew talking right on the other side. There were a lot of other conversations going on inside the room, as Jackie was waiting to start the meeting, but I was only concentrated on this one conversation. Maria sat next to me and tried to steal my attention away from what was going on outside, but my ears didn't leave the conversation. It was hard to fully make out what was being said, but I could still make out most of their conversation. I kept hearing Drew say something along the lines of "Why are you going here? Why do you still hang around Ethan?" and Tom would reply with "It's no big deal, I can come here if I want, Crystal's my friend." I tried keeping my cool and just kept listening, and then I heard Drew say "His friends were talking about him taking you to some masquerade party later this year. You know what this means right? He likes you, I told you to watch your back for this sort of thing". At that point, I jumped up and went outside to join the conversation, and a concerned Maria came right after me. I went right in between Drew and Tom, turned to Drew and said, "If there's anything you wanna say about me I'm right here, you don't need to involve my friends." Tom and Maria backed up a little, knowing I had what it took to defend myself, but stayed close by just in case, because we noticed that today, there was no security guard.

"He's not your friend, he's mine, and I know what you freaks are all about. I'm trying to protect him," said Drew. He said this with an aggressive tone, but I could still sense the fear in his voice as if he was scared of me. I, on the other hand, made sure to show nothing but aggression as I said to him "Instead of worrying about me and who I'm friends with, why don't you focus on your own relationship?" Drew snickered at me and said, "You know, maybe you're right. After all, I'd rather be with a real girl who doesn't have to fake it". As he said this, his hand went onto my chest, and I almost became paralyzed with fear. Out of reflex, I slapped him hard enough that it echoed in the empty hallway. There was a silence as all four of us were shocked by what had just happened. Drew looked at me angrily as he rubbed his now red cheek.

"What's going on?" said Jackie, coming outside to check on us. Drew ran down a nearby stairwell, as Jackie approached me. "That slap was so hard, we heard it from inside," she said to me. Then she smiled and put her hand on my arm "Good job." Jackie hugged me and walked me back inside.

So moral of the story, Drew needs to leave me and my friends alone, or next time it'll be a lot more than a simple slap across the face

TRACY'S PHONE

Anna: Hey Mom, there's something I found out that I felt I should tell you.

Tracy: I'm home, you can't say it to me in person?

Anna: I'm at Drews. It's about Ethan.

Tracy: What's so important about him?

Anna: Did he ask you for money recently?

Tracy: Actually, he asked for $10 a couple of days ago. Why?

Anna: Oh no.

Tracy: What? He said it was for a field trip or something.

Anna: When did he say the trip was?

Tracy: I don't remember.

Anna: Was it March 25th?

Tracy: I don't know, what does it matter?

Anna: March 25th there's gonna be a party, it's at a gay hang out. I believe it's mostly adults too, so who knows what Ethan's trying to get involved in.

Tracy: Even though Ethan's strangely flamboyant, I don't imagine he'd wanna get involved in that crowd. He's a pretty shy kid

Anna: I heard him say he wanted to go.

Tracy: Are you sure?

Anna: It's best I told you now.

Tracy: I'll find out what's going on.

Anna: You're welcome.

December 1st

12:19 PM

Tracy: Where are you? Why aren't you home?

Ethan: I went to the mall with Maria. I'm actually on my way home now.

Tracy: What was up at the mall?

Ethan: A sale at the crafts store.

Tracy: Uh huh.
Tracy: So what museum are you going to on the 25th?

Ethan: Actually, I'm not gonna head home right now. I'm going to Maria's.

Tracy: Anna told me about a party at a gay hangout, with adults, and that you were actually interested in going?
Tracy: Did you lie to me, Ethan? Not only lie to me but use my money for something you knew I would disapprove of? What has gotten into you?

Ethan: It's a masquerade ball, it's hosted by the Pride Center, it's an event for high school students.

Tracy: You will come right home from school every day and clean the entire house up and down, and you will not leave my sight!
Tracy: And I expect my $10 back.
Tracy: Answer me! Do you understand what I'm telling you?

Ethan: Yes.

ANNA'S PHONE

December 1st

12:43 PM

Ethan: What you did was really fucked up. This is a new low, even for you.

Anna: I don't know what you're talking about.

Ethan: Give it up! Why is it your life goal to make me miserable? Is a night out with people who understand and accept me so much to ask for?

Anna: You lied to my mom, and you're facing the consequences for it. Man up.
Anna: Oh, and since you're grounded, my room can use a good dusting, and my laundries backed up. Thanks, babe.

Ethan: Fuck you, Anna.

Anna: <3

I remember everything. I remember seeing an ice skating show when I was 3. I remember wearing a red jacket. I remember my mom was holding me. I remember my whole family being there. I remember how I was so intimidated because they were all so much bigger than me.

I remember being the smallest one at the dinner table every night. I remember how that inspired me to make my presence as big as possible. I remember just making up stories and rambling on at four years old. I sometimes remember when my family encouraged me. I remember other times when they just wanted to be left alone.

I remember every time I was told: "You can't do this with us because you're too young." I remember every time my family would watch TV in the family room together and I was left to my toys in the other room.

Wicked Stepmothers will always try to maintain the image of a perfect family. It's like I was being taught to always bottle it up and that showing vulnerability would ruin that image, which seems pretty funny now since my most vulnerable moments were in that beautiful but broken household. The things that truly broke me were the mind games that were played revolving around this concept of love. All she would ever talk to me about is how I missed a spot cleaning the counter or didn't do the laundry right. And when she starts going off, she takes her precious time to stop. It'll go from the spot on the counter to the stain on her shirt from last week, then about how I should be more focused on doing what she says than homework or school, then how I'm a nuisance and a burden, and eventually back to the spot on the counter. And as much as I want to walk away, I'm stuck sitting through her rant every single time. So, I do as I'm told, say what she wants to hear, and carry on. But every single time it takes another toll on me. Always trying to tiptoe around her, fearing whatever reaction I get from her, was all mentally exhausting. But then it would always end with "But I Love You."

I remember every toy I ever had. I remember the yellow toy truck. I remember the dolls. I remember the excitement over holidays like Christmas and Halloween. I remember every family gathering. I remember feeling lost in a big crowd of bigger people. I remember how it started feeling easier and easier to just fade away. I remember when it started to feel like no one was missing me in my own family.

I always felt like the outsider in my family because I was separated from my stepsisters by age. I never really got to experience having my own siblings to grow up with. It hurt growing up constantly feeling below everyone else. My wicked stepmother never wanted me to show vulnerability. Meanwhile, that entire family saw me, made me completely vulnerable. I'm expected to simply get over and accept being called a "Lost Cause" & "Worthless," being threatened with a hammer, being grabbed by the neck, hit in the head. What sticks with me the most is being taken out of the shower and held out of the doorway of the house with only a wet towel covering me while being threatened to get thrown out. A family should be the security for a young child. I did my best to become the best person I could be with or without that security. The Wicked Stepmother & Ugly Stepsisters were never worth the dismay of a queen. Especially with a ball to attend…

Scene 9: School Hallway

(Lights go on. Outside their lockers, Maria approaches Crystal, dressed as Ethan.)

Maria: Hey! Did you ask your stepmom about the ball?

Crystal: Yeah. I can't go.

Maria: Aww, why?

Crystal: (lying) Not enough money.

Maria: That sucks.

Crystal: I'm not going to lie. I was kind of looking forward to it.

Maria: You only needed $10, right?

Crystal: Yeah.

(Maria takes out $10 and puts it down Crystal's shirt)

Crystal: Maria, you don't have to.

Maria: Yeah, yeah, I know. I want this to work out for you. After school today, let's go to the mall, we'll get you a dress, shoes, even a mask.

Crystal: Maria, I don't know what to say. This is so sweet of you. Thank you. But, how do I get around Tracy?

Maria: We can say you're spending the night at my house. She likes me anyway.

Crystal: That'll work.

Maria: See… I told you it would all work out. Now, let's go get you that dress!

(Maria and Crystal hold hands and exit)

Fairy God Mothers are very special beings that appear to you when you need them the most, and often when you least expect it. They appear to you when you've lost hope entirely. Even when they make the presence known, it's hard to accept the reality of things finally going your way because you're just so used to everything going wrong. What's funny is that I've always known my fairy godmother was with me, since I was little. I've always seen my fairy godmother in my best friends. But the most memorable time was through someone in my own family, my real godmother. I was 13 years old. I was in 8th grade, my last year of middle school. Even though middle school was wrapping up, I still experienced bullying. Not as horrific as 6th and 7th grade. There was a group of boys who had this disturbing obsession with me. I was abused by them day after day, and when I went to the dean, a careless, corrupt, despicable man, all he ever said was "Bullies have rights." Eventually, the bullying died down, but the effects of their actions were still rippling, and other bullies continued the job. Even the littlest insult took me back to that traumatic experience. I felt alone. I was still here in a physical body, going to school, getting shit done, but my spirit, my hope all fell deep down into a dark hole. I know I'm not the only one who's been through this, some go through worse, some don't even live to tell the tale. I do not say this to pull sympathy; I only say it to educate about what bullying really does. I tried to kill myself at this time. I was brought home from school and told I couldn't legally go back without getting a psychiatric evaluation. I felt alone, like no one in that house would've missed me either way, until one person came forward. My godmother. We went on a car ride, and I wasn't sure where we were going. We parked in front of a school. It was where she went to middle school. She told me about when she got bullied when she was followed home when she was threatened and how it affected her. When the topic came up of what I had done, all she said to me was

"That pain we all went through when grandma died, would've been so much worse if something happened to you. This family would not be whole without you. This family would be broken without you. We need you."

No one had ever gone out of their way like that for me before that point. In one of my darkest moments, my fairy godmother appeared to me exactly the way I imagined. Through a strong-willed, determined woman, who's been through just as much hurt as anyone else, but never let it stop her from doing what she wants, and never let it touch her everlasting smile. A woman who would become a role model and an inspiration to me. A woman who I ultimately owe my life. From that point, she would frequently check up on me, and to this day makes sure I have someone to talk to and that I never feel alone. But no one, not even a fairy godmother, can fully shut out all the hatred and pain in this world. No one is that powerful.

Scene 10: Mall

(Maria and Crystal are at a dress boutique in the mall. Maria is waiting outside of the dressing room for Crystal.)

Maria: Come on, Crystal, I feel like I've been waiting an hour!

Crystal: Then wait for another one! (A couple of seconds pass) Okay, I think I'm ready (Comes out in a pink dress) What do you think?

Maria: I don't know, I don't see you in pink. You would look so much better in blue.

Crystal: I love this on me. I'm getting it…wait outside for me. (Enters fitting room.)

(Anna comes into the store and sees Maria.)

Anna: (Approaches Maria with a phony demeanor) Hey Maria, how are you?

Maria: (Rolling her eyes) Oh, hey Anna.

Anna: (Gets as close as she can to Maria) I didn't know you shop here.

Maria: (Stepping away from Anna) I don't, I'm here with Crystal.

Anna: You know, she's been spending lots of time with your cousin, Tom. Ugh, he's such a dream.

Maria: (Gags) Ew!

Anna: So, what does Crystal think of him? It's almost impossible to spend so much time with someone as charming as him and not have a crush on him.

Maria: It's not my place to talk to you about this.

Anna: Oh, I know you're dying to talk about it. So, do they have a thing or what?

Maria: (Takes a step away from Anna) I keep telling Crystal to make things work with him, but she's too nervous, despite her giant obsession with him.

(Crystal looks away while Anna pulls out her phone and presses record.)

Anna: Would you really call it an obsession?

Maria: (Still not facing Anna, moving her hands as she speaks) Well, a big giant crush.

(Crystal comes out of the dressing area and in a new outfit with her new dress in hand.)

Crystal: (To Anna) Oh I didn't know you shop here. I just figured you go to the lost and found and hope you get lucky.

Anna: Wow, you're so hilarious. What's the dress for? Why waste so much money on something so unflattering?

Crystal: This dress is beautiful.

Anna: It is! It just looks unflattering on men. Let me guess it's for your magical masquerade ball...

Crystal: Yes, it is, where I am going to wear it, look amazing, and have a magical night.

Anna: That sounds great (takes out dark lipstick) it would just be a shame if (Smears lipstick on the dress) Oops. My bad. (As she is exiting) Well, have a good time at your ball!

Crystal: What am I going to do now?

Maria: Let me tell you something about us (air quotes) "fairy godmothers." We always have a backup plan.

(Crystal and Maria exit.)

The story of the blue dress is nothing too extravagant. Dress shopping is something I enjoyed doing with my best friend from high school. She took me with her one day after school for early prom dress shopping. No one seemed to care about the fact that I was a boy trying on dresses. No one except for me at least. But my best friend stayed right by my side like she did throughout everything else, we tried on gowns, took pictures, looked stunning, laughed, and had a good time. Although this was something I wanted to do, go out and shop for prom dresses, it was scary finally doing it. But she was with me to make it a memory that I hold near and dear to my heart. I guess that was my fairy godmother making a reappearance. I ended up wearing black to prom. She wore blue. It was always her favorite color. She's someone else who I've seen go through a lot of hurt and make it out on the other end with nothing but strength and glowing infectious smile. It was impossible to be in any bad mood around her. I would've never made it throughout that shitshow called high school without her.

I actually had two blue dresses, both for my very first two shows putting this story on stage. Both from the dress shop, I ended up working at after high school and throughout college. The blue dress from the first show, a flowing periwinkle gown with straps falling off the shoulders, and a high slit with the flowing piece of light blue fabric trailing behind my legs. From the second show, a two-piece azure gown, the top decorated in a floral design and covered in jewels, and a full princess skirt covering my legs entirely that looked magical when I spun around.

Wearing these dresses, I sent my character, Crystal, off to the ball to meet with her Prince Charming.

TOM'S PHONE

Crystal: Hey! I can't wait for tonight!

Tom: Same here!

Crystal: I'm getting ready with Maria now and then we're going to the pride center. You wanna meet us outside?

Tom: Sure!

Crystal: Alright, I'll see you then. Let me know when you get there!

Tom: Will do!

March 25th

4:30 PM

Maria: You better not chicken out tonight.

Tom: Pardon me?

Maria: You need to tell Crystal how you feel about her. You're not gonna stop feeling so badly about it unless you tell her and get it off your chest tonight.

Tom: You don't think I'm hoping to? I just know that when the moment comes, it'll be a lot harder than just saying it in my head or writing it on paper.

Maria: It's like pulling off a band-aid dude, you just gotta do it. Just say the first words "Crystal I need to admit something to you," and it'll just get easier as it goes.

Tom: I've thought about every possibility of what she'll say to me. But I still don't think I'm fully prepared for what could happen.

Maria: I promise you, whatever her reaction is it won't be negative. She's not a heartbreaker. At some point tonight, sooner than later, you guys can go outside to the garden, alone, and you can tell her.

Tom: Thank you, Maria.

Maria: Always. Let's have a good time tonight!

Scene 12: THE BALL

(Lights go on; Tom waits for the girls outside the ballroom, wearing a mostly white suit. There are decorations and people walking in, as Crystal and Maria both enter.)

Maria: (To Tom, excitedly) Hi!

Tom: (Kindly) Hey you look great. (Hugs Maria.)

Maria: (Her eyes are lit with confidence). Thanks!

Tom: (To Crystal) Wow, so this is what you look like when you're not in black…

Crystal: (Giggling) Is that a compliment?

Tom: Yeah, you look beautiful.

Crystal: Thanks, you look great too.

Maria: Yeah, yeah, let's continue this inside. (Pushing the two aside) I smell the food from out here.

(Stage lights are dim. The spotlight is on Crystal, Tom, and Maria as they enter stage left.)

Crystal: (Turning around) This is so stupid.

Maria: (Stopping her) You are not leaving until you two fall in love.

Tom: What?

Crystal: Don't mind her. I need fresh air. You want to step outside?

Tom: Sure.

(They exit.)

(Drew and Anna see Crystal and Tom together.)

Anna: (Eyes rolling) That freak really is here, and our star athlete is her date.

Drew: This is unbelievable! What's the plan?

Anna: Just wait till midnight, (Pulling out her phone) then this starts playing...

Drew: What is it?

Anna: Maria admitting Crystal's thirsty for Tom. Just get me to the loudspeaker.

Maria: (Noticing Anna and Drew) What are you guys doing here? This is for GSA only.

Anna: We just want to warn Tom about Crystal's crush. Just wait until midnight

(Anna exits with Drew. Maria runs off after Anna. Crystal and Tom talk outside.)

CRYSTAL'S PHONE

March 25th

10:01 PM

Maria: Crystal, where are you?

Crystal: Sorry, we've been outside for a while, we're gonna come back in soon.

Maria: A while?

Crystal: Oh, come on, we've been in and out.

Maria: Look, there's something going on, I think we need to leave, and it needs to be before midnight.

Crystal: What are you going off about?

Maria: Crystal. Anna's here.

Crystal: How is that possible?

Maria: I don't know, she's here with Drew, she said something was gonna happen at midnight.

Crystal: Maria, even if that was her, she was probably just talking about when she's gonna leave.

Maria: Crystal gets serious. Why is she even here?

102

Crystal: Don't know, don't care, I'm having an amazing time and no one's gonna mess that up.

Maria: I know, and I'm happy for you, but I just have a bad feeling.
Maria: Let's just leave early, before midnight, to be safe.

Crystal: Considering how tonight's going, I'd rather stay till the end.

Maria: What even have you and Tom been doing?

Crystal: Nothing you gotta worry about. Worry about your own date.

Maria: I'm sorry, who put clothes on your back tonight?

Crystal: Why do you feel the need to throw it in my face?
Crystal: Look, you've been telling me to be positive about this ball since it was announced, and I'm finally doing that, so why try to mess it up?

Maria: I'm not the one trying to mess it up!
Maria: Honestly, whatever,, I'll see you inside.

Scene 12 continued

Tom: So I've always wanted to ask (almost choking on his words, nervous to ask) how is it dating as a trans teenager?

Crystal: Any guy I ever liked was either straight, 18 or over, in a relationship, a total jerk, or a combination of all four. What about you?

Tom: I had a couple of girlfriends before I realized. But now I'm just confused.

Crystal: How's that whole thing going?

Tom: I don't know, I haven't told anyone else. What was it like coming out at home?

Crystal: Yeah, about that, I have a stepmom who is impossible to talk to. I never got the opportunity to know my birth mother.

Tom: Well if she's anything like you at least you know she was beautiful.

~

Tom: We've been outside for a while. Do you want to go back inside?

Crystal: Gladly.

(The two go back inside as slow music plays. The piano's being played on stage.)

Crystal: A slow song. Perfect timing.

Tom: May I have this dance? (Holds out his hand.)

Crystal: I can't dance for shit...

Tom: Just trust me.

(Tom, moving to the music, takes her to the center of the dance floor as the people in the background leave the stage.)

Crystal: Oh god, you know what you're doing.

Tom: You don't?

Crystal: This is my first slow dance, ever.

Tom: Well, I'll try to make it memorable for you. (spins her)

Crystal: Am I red?

Tom: Little bit.

ANNA'S PHONE

March 25th

11: 38 PM

Drew: Anna, where the hell did you go now?

Anna: I wanted to see where he was, he came back inside, and he's dancing with Tom.

Drew: Who, Ethan?

Anna: Who else?
Anna: I'm coming back now, when I do, I want you to read what I gave you on the loudspeaker after the audio plays.

Drew: What, this book?

Anna: Have you looked at it?

Drew: No, there's a lot of confusion I'm trying to get past first.
Drew: What is this, a diary?

Anna: Yeah. I bookmarked the page for you to read.

Drew: This is Ethan's, isn't it?
Drew: And the bookmarked page is him talking about his feelings for Tom?

106

Anna: Yeah.

Drew: Anna, I am not doing this, I don't care how much I don't like the kid, he's a human. Now that I've seen the way he expresses himself in his writing, that's even more clear to me now.

Drew: This is completely heartless, and I'm not doing it. What has he ever done to you? He's your stepbrother.

Anna: You really think you can just back out of this now? What are you gonna do, expose me to the entire football team? It's not like anyone would ever listen to what you have to say.

Anna: Meanwhile, you and I both know I know a lot about you, including the specific reason why you hate Ethan and any other "fag" as you would say. And our student body has a history of believing even the most outrageous lie I tell. I'm sure they'd believe the truth just the same.

Drew: What kind of evil person would threaten something like that? You're talking about something that was traumatic for me, and you're just gonna shove it in my face like that?

Anna: Yeah, I am.

Anna: When I get back to the room you're gonna read the diary entry on the loudspeaker, names and all, and then you're free to go home.

Anna: Okay, Baby?

Drew: Okay...

THE GROUP CHAT

March 26th

12:00 AM

Jackie: Hey, I ended up leaving about 20 minutes ago. Are all you guys okay getting home?

Gus: Jackie, you missed something crazy.
Gus: Everyone was getting ready to leave, and Crystal and Tom were dancing together, it was really cute.
Gus: But then this audio came on the loudspeaker, it sounded like Maria, and she was talking about how much Crystal liked Tom. Then there was this guy reading what sounded like a love letter. The name Tom was used, and it very much resembled the way Crystal writes and talks.

Jackie: Oh no, was she okay?

Gus: Crystal ran off, and Tom ran after her, we don't know what happened after that.

Luke: And you know, that guy reading it sounded like Drew.

Gus: Who?

Luke: I don't know his last name. He was on the football team with Tom at some point.

Gus: You don't think Tom had something to do with it?

Jackie: Gus, really? You know Crystal's in this group chat.
Jackie: Does anyone know where they are now?

Suzy: Maria ran after her too, she texted me saying she found Tom but doesn't know where Crystal went.

Jackie: Just keep me updated.

Gus: Got you

Luke: No problem.

Suzy: Of course.

Gus: Well tonight really was legendary after all...

CRYSTAL'S PHONE

March 26th

12:01 AM

Maria: Crystal? Where did you go?
Maria: Please answer. I'm freaking out!
Maria: What was that thing being read on the loudspeaker? Did you write that?
Maria: Where are you?
Maria: Crystal, seriously this isn't funny.
Maria: Crystal!!
Maria: I called you, like five times.
Maria: Please just don't do anything stupid.
Maria: I love you, please know that.

March 26th

12:01 AM

Tom: Crystal, where are you?

Tom: Seriously, I'm looking all over for you!

Tom: What was that on the loudspeaker?

Tom: Crystal, after what we experienced tonight, how we connected, what we learned about each other, how can you just run away from me?

Tom: Please know that everything you feel, especially in that message on the loudspeaker, don't be ashamed of it. I feel the same way.

Tom: Just please let me know if you're okay.

March 26th

11:04 AM

Jackie: Hey, love. I heard about what happened last night. I left early, so I didn't actually see or hear anything. I get why you ran off, but we were all so worried about you. I came back to help find you. I can't imagine what you're going through, and I don't wanna say something like, "Oh, I know what you're going through." I don't. I can't understand what it's like to go through what you go through. But know that I want to help. A lot of people care about you and want you to be okay. I can't expect you to answer; you deserve a day to just rest and breathe. It's not the end of the world, today's a new day, tomorrow's a new day, and Monday starts a new week. Hang in there; you're a strong person I know you'll be okay. Just know that I'm supporting you no matter what. Stay strong boo.

Jackie: Oh, and I might as well let you know, elections for next year's GSA president start next month, early May the latest. I better see you running!

Act 2 Scene 5: Crystal's House

(Anna enters)

Crystal: Hey Sis

Anna: I thought the deal was we don't acknowledge each other at home.

Crystal: Considering recent events, I think we can make an exception.

Anna: What about names, are you Crystal or Ethan today?

Crystal: Names aren't important.

Anna: So your sassy sarcasm has returned. How inspirational, bullied tranny rises from the ashes!

Crystal: Enough! As if it's not enough for me to have a stepmother and stepsister forced into my life. Why do you act this way? What have I ever done to you? We could've had a beautiful relationship.

Anna: You think your life is so miserable, don't you? See, these are the things I can't stand about you; you make everything about you, do you think it was easy for me? To have a new stepbrother but lose him because he became my stepsister!

Crystal: So that's why you hate me?

Anna: Not entirely. Who would want to be my friend after learning that our school's freak is my family? You're nothing but a burden to me.

Crystal: So that's what it's all about? Your own conceited self-image. What, you thought Tom was going to like you because you're Miss Perfect? Hate to break it to you, but I made it with him a bit further than you did.

Anna: Oh please, do you really think Tom is anything special? Every guy you've known has hurt you whether they've bullied you or broke your heart, Tom is no different.

Crystal: (Shrugging her shoulders) Do you really expect me to listen to you?

Anna: Open your eyes. Remember how you used to cry when boys would bully you, or your newest crush turned out to be straight or was mean to you? You've fooled yourself to believe Tom is different.

Crystal: (Stepping up to Anna) He is different. Even if I get hurt, isn't that what you want?

Anna: I'm trying to help you. He's playing you. Remember who said once in middle school, "The perfect guy only exists in fairy tales?" Where did that quote come from? Oh yeah, from you. I know you've had doubts about Tom…

Crystal: (Upset) Of course I have. I don't want to believe he's like that…

Anna: It's time you accept it. (Shows Crystal her phone.) Because Drew sent me this last night...

Crystal: What is it?

Anna: Something Tom said while texting Drew.

Crystal: (Reading the text messages) "He's so clingy and ugly. He can't even realize how embarrassing he really looks, or acts. Overall, he's a freak."

Anna: (Taking her phone back) See what I mean?

Crystal: (Shaking her head) He wouldn't say that.

Anna: Wouldn't he?

(Crystal runs off upset, and Anna walks away with a grin on her face)

Crystal & Therapist

"How do you feel?"

"Tired"

"How much sleep have you been getting?"

"Enough"

"Are you sure?"

"I think."

"What are you feeling right now?"

"Calm"

"Tired calm?"

"Peaceful calm."

"What do you want the most right now?"

"Sleep"

"What do you want the most out of life?"

"Success"

"Do you feel like you're on your way?"

"Yes"

"How do you know?"

"I've been working hard."

"But is there still more you can be doing?"

"Pass"

"What do you hate the most?"

"Social Interaction"

"Why?"

"It's just... I don't know... it's annoying."

"But what makes it annoying?"

"Look, maybe this just isn't for me. I have to go, goodbye."

CRYSTAL'S DIARY

After we walked in and as the night started to move forward, Tom and I walked outside in the garden. We've had many conversations, many kind words to say to each other. But I could tell this time he had put down almost every wall around him. Walls I didn't even realize were there. He talked about his parents and how they carried an image of the man they wanted him to be, expecting him to grow into a pillar of society. But he carried all the baggage of a part of him that he was taught not to embrace. He's lived his whole life without allowing even his parents to know his true self. And here I am writing about someone else's problems in my as if it's my struggle. But that's just how much I care for him.

After walking through this otherworldly garden, we felt a sense of relief as we finally found a bench to rest on. We sat next to each other, he asked me about how dating was for me, then when the topic switched to his dating life, it led to him asking me how it was coming out at home. "I'm not out to my parents. Or at least what's left of them," I replied. I then went on to tell him the sob story of my cold stepmother. "I never got the chance to know my mother," I said. And he replied, "If she's anything like you, at least you know she was beautiful." We were sitting next to each other, coming closer with every word that we spoke until we were touching. We looked at each other. I looked right into his dark eyes, getting lost in them. And the next moment, we were kissing.

Not much talking from that point, but it wasn't needed. We were alone in a secluded garden, where everyone else was inside. I wasn't afraid of what was happening. No, it didn't go that far, I mean we were both looking polished as hell, and we weren't about to mess ourselves up then. And all I had to do afterward was retouch my lipstick and fix my hair. And help him wipe off the lipstick from his face... And neck. I mean, it sure wasn't my first kiss, and it wasn't the first boy I felt like I was in love with. But this is the first time where it felt genuine. With Tom, I felt like I didn't have to question anything

Tom

The Second Piece of Inspiration

Like I said before, Tom is based on two people. First, the boy from the bus stop. The second, the boy from the dance. I've known him since my freshman year of high school; ironically, he was dating another friend of mine at the time. A girl. We were never that close. Never really connected. Never really had the opportunity to get to know each other. That is until senior year came around. He would sit with me and my friends at lunch since he was a good friend of my best friend, the one I went dress shopping with. From there, we started hanging out more and became closer as friends, but there was definitely an unspoken attraction. From what I knew, he was straight, so I didn't push or cross any boundaries. He, on the other hand, got very handsy at times when he shouldn't. But my attraction to him let it be.

In high school, there was something me and my friends celebrated once a year called Gay Prom. We called it Gay Prom at least. It was the Pride Center's Youth Prom, a part of their week of pride events. Year after year it was a fun night out with friends and getting to meet other queer students from across the island. My first year, freshman year, I went without permission, behind the stepmothers back, with the help of my friends. As seniors, we were ready to go out with a bang. And because I'm a dumbass, I invited him to come with us.

We went, me, my Maria, & my Tom. He was friendly and open with everyone there. But at one point he seemed taken back when someone came onto him. We went to be alone for a little, and he opened up to me about his struggles with his own sexual identity. So then the night progressed, we danced together for a little while, made out in the hallway for a longer while. And as quickly as it built up and progressed, it began to unravel. My best friend and fairy godmother saw us kissing and seemed hurt by me as if I was disrespecting her by kissing him. He then quickly withdrew and took himself back, saying something had merely come over him, and it was a misunderstanding. They both ignored me for the rest of the night.

The following week at school was humiliating. All of a sudden, the Monday we went back, he had a girlfriend. And also a lot of people knew what had happened at Gay Prom. People I didn't even talk to, including his new girlfriend. I felt used. I was used. I felt betrayed by my best friend. She eventually told me how she felt uncomfortable around us because she couldn't forget the image of us kissing. It's easy to assume she liked him, but I don't want to assume that. She's an incredible woman; someone like him wouldn't be deserving of her.

So the true story isn't exactly Crystal & Tom's love story in my play, but if you really thought my story was gonna be about heartbreak and turmoil over not getting the prince and giving up on all hopes of a happy ending…

Oh bitch. Get ready for the plot twist.

ANNA'S PHONE

March 28th

7:08 AM

Anna: OMG, you guys are never gonna believe what Tom told me.

Shay: OMG, what?

Steph: What's up??

Anna: He totally made out with Ethan at a party Friday night.

Steph: OMG, no way!

Shay: He told you??

Anna: He was basically bragging about it.

Shay: Ugh, that's gross.

Anna: I know, right?
Anna: Just don't talk about it to anyone.

Steph: Yeah, of course!

Shay: Your secret is safe with us!

THE CHEERLEADERS GROUP CHAT

March 28th

7:09 AM

Shay: OMG, you guys are not gonna believe what Anna just told us!!

Steph: Tom hooked up with Ethan at a party on Friday and is basically going around bragging about it.

Erika: What?? That's so messed up.

Didi: That's so awful, guys are disgusting.

Steph: I can't imagine what Ethan's going through...

Erika: Didn't he change his name to Crystal or something?

Shay: I just can't believe someone as hot as him would stoop low enough to someone like that.

Didi: And then brag about it like it's something to be proud of?

Erika: BRB, I'm gonna spread the word.

THE JOCKS GROUP CHAT

March 28th

7:12 AM

Cole: So, Tom is a part of the "LGBTQXYZBLT" community now, and it's all thanks to that freak.

Frank: No way! Ethan seriously got to him?
Frank: It's a known fact you can't even make eye contact with that kid, his eyes alone are so creepy under all that makeup.

John: I swear I've wanted to ring that freaks neck since 6th grade.

Cole: Especially now.

Frank: Not like it'd be difficult. John could kill that kid with one flick.

John: Don't give me a challenge. I'd knock the gay right out of him and Tom if I got the chance.

TOM'S PHONE

March 28th

7:42 AM

Maria: Hey...

Tom: Yeah, I know, everyone's talking about Crystal and me kissing at the masquerade ball.
Tom: The cheerleaders were saying I was bragging about kissing her, so now I don't know what's going around about me...

Maria: I was actually just gonna ask you if you did the English homework, but we can talk about that if you want.

.

Tom: I don't think I wanna do sports at all anymore. The whole team blocked me.

Maria: Because that's all they can do. Look at how weak this generation is, unfollowing or blocking someone on any social media account is the worst thing anyone would do. People are gonna talk, give it a week, and they'll be over it.

Tom: But I don't want all of this being spread. I didn't say a word to anyone, why is everyone saying I was bragging about kissing her?

126

Maria: I know no one from GSA would've said anything about it. Who else was there?

Tom: Oh, I know.

Tom added Drew to the chat

Maria: OOF.

Tom: Do you wanna explain your role in this?

Drew: Sure. In person, and not in a group chat with a girl I barely know.

Maria: This girl you barely know is best friends with both Tom and Crystal.

Drew: Look, I promise this isn't my fault.

Tom: Was it you reading Crystal's diary over the loudspeaker or not?

Drew: Yes, it was, but I can explain.
Drew: Someone blackmailed me into doing it.

Tom: Blackmailed you? Who?

Drew added Anna to the chat

127

Anna: Hi.

Tom: Anna, did you blackmail Drew into reading Crystal's diary over the loudspeaker at the dance, then spread a rumor saying I was bragging about kissing her?

Anna: Yeah.
Anna: Why?

Maria: How did you guys even get in?

Anna: It wasn't that hard, we just snuck in through the back and hid in the utility room.
Anna: But I didn't blackmail Drew until right before it happened. He willingly snuck into the ballroom with me.

Drew: You didn't even explain to me what you would be doing until the last minute, you just kept saying, "follow me, trust me, babe."

Tom: Either way, you both did what you did!

Drew: Bro, I swear I didn't wanna do it.

Tom: Shut up, Drew!
Tom: Why would you do all of this?

Anna: I was mad at him.

Drew: Okay, I get a lot's going on right now but has anyone spoken to Crystal? How is she? Is she okay?

Anna: ...

                                        Tom: ???

Maria: *gasp*

Drew: What?

Maria: You just referred to Crystal by her preferred name

                        Tom: And the preferred pronoun

Drew: Yeah, and? Isn't that what you're supposed to do?

            Tom: It is, it's just surprising seeing you do it.

Drew: Give me a break, I'm new to this whole "being an ally" thing.

Maria: What twisted parallel universe am I in right now??

            Tom: I can't imagine how upset she'll be when she realizes the whole student body is talking about what happened at the ball...

Maria: She probably already knows.

Anna: Omg you guys know she's already in school, right?

Anna: I just saw her breaking the dress code any way possible and in some dramatic makeup. She didn't acknowledge any of the laughter and whispering going on around her.

Maria: Where did you see her?

Anna: On the 2nd floor. As usual, she was the center of attention, especially now. She seems to be enjoying it more than ever.

CRYSTAL'S PHONE

March 28th

1:50 PM

Jackie: Hey Crystal.

Crystal: Hey! What's up?

Jackie: How have you been doing since Friday night?

Crystal: Really good actually, especially today.

Jackie: That's good. Why, especially today?

Crystal: Just in a good mood today.

Jackie: You seem to be handling everything really well.

Crystal: There's nothing major to handle.

Jackie: You really are unshakable, aren't you?

Crystal: I may have had a moment at the ball, but everyone has their moments.
Crystal: BTW, I'm so sorry I worried you that night.

Jackie: No, it's fine! You're remarkably confident. That's a very big trait that the president of GSA should have.

Crystal: OMG, thank you, that means so much!
Crystal: Any updates on when the election starts?

Jackie: Just make sure you're at the next meeting <3

Crystal: Will do, see you there!!

TOM'S NOTEBOOK

Dear Crystal,

Truthfully, I really don't know what there is to say.

I mean, there is a lot I want to say, but once again, I can't bring myself to even write it down. Whenever I've done this before, the only thoughts I have to let out for you are positive. This time that's not the case. But I'm still gonna do my best.

I felt like I was walking in your shoes today. Wherever I was, someone was staring or laughing or whispering about me. My friends don't know what to do when they see me. You, on the other hand, went off, smiling and waving at every crowd that would yell or laugh at you. Even in a crowd you still stand out to me the most, but whenever you saw me, I got a quick stare, and you would just, keep going.

So, is that it now? We kiss, I felt something for you that I haven't felt for anyone else, and now that the words out about our kiss you're using it as a way to get more attention then you already get? Now you wanna treat me like a total stranger? I've said this over and over, but I'm not as tough as you are. You're able to have the entire class know all about you and harass you over it, and you're enjoying every second of it. I'm not like that; I don't take that kind of judgment and ridicule as easily. You're using your disadvantage to your advantage. But my disadvantage isn't that I can't brush off the bullying of my peers. It's that despite the way you're acting now, I still love you. And I have no clue how to take advantage of that.

I guess we all do and feel things without fully knowing why. And I hope that's why you're being as cold as you are. I trust you're adult enough to get past this.

Tom

In the darkness, I see nothing. Yet I convince myself I see everything there is to see, or at least that I think there is to see. It's always been so easy for me to manipulate my brain to see anything I could think of. It's so easy to tell myself there's someone in this dark room with me and the only reason as to why I can't see them is because it's too dark. Just because you don't see it, it doesn't take away from the possibility of its reality. It's easy to believe any thought that comes to my head. It's been a gift, as I've been able to bring amazing ideas and concepts into reality and create beautiful things. But that same gift has also been a curse. Anything I choose to believe, I will, including the bad. If I think someone doesn't like me, they don't. If I think someone's saying something bad about me, they are. If I think I'm unwanted, I am.

In the shadows is where the darkest creatures lurk. The ones that don't want to be seen because of their own fears. Because they believe they're too ugly, too awkward, or too weird to come out and be seen. So the shadows are the safest place for them to stay. But maybe what they believe isn't true. Maybe they are beautiful. Maybe they are valid. But the perceptions of those around you can create a whole different reality. That is if you allow them to.

My Island is home to the third biggest high school in America, where the only two colors in existence are purple and white. From my own experience in this school, I can tell you it's a breeding ground for young bigots, being raised to carry on the traditions of a red island in a blue state. Fortunately, some lost souls

135

manage to fall through the cracks and deviate from the expected closed-mindedness. And by lost souls, I mean the ones who dare to be different. Those who are brave enough not to let what they grew up in shape their morals. All the way at the North Shore of the island is the Pride Center. The one small but real resource for queer youth in a community where most of the parents are too old fashioned and ignorant to be having kids. But no matter how small, they offer a safe place for the kids who feel too scared to be themselves in their own homes.

Act 2 Scene 3: Bus Stop

(School is over. Anna confronts Crystal)

Anna: Nice to see you had the balls to come to school today.

Crystal: (Trying to walk away) Not now, Anna.

Anna: (Stopping her) Where do you think you're going?

(Tom and Drew enter.)

Tom: (To Anna) Leave her alone, Anna, what has she ever done to you?

Anna: A lot more than you'd think. Right, Ethan?

(Crystal turns around defensively, and they collide. Tom drags Anna off stage, while Drew grabs Crystal, who escapes his grip.)

Crystal: Let go of me! Go away!

Drew: (Hesitates) Are you okay?

Crystal: Did you not hear me the first time? Leave jockstrap!

Drew: (Pause) I'm sorry.

Crystal: What?

Drew: (Nervously) I'm sorry for how I've treated you in the past.

Crystal: What game are you playing?

Drew: It's not a game; it's the truth.

Crystal: Yeah, right.

Drew: If I may ask, only because I'm concerned (Pause) why did you snap at Anna? You've seemed fine all day

Crystal: (Eyes are fiery) As if I owe you an explanation.

Drew: Well, no one else is around to listen, except me.

Crystal: (Hesitating and pausing) Look at how being trans affects me. I get bullied, judged, threatened; I don't get along with my stepmom because of it, I'm late to class every day because I can't get dressed at home. And now I love someone who's never going to love me back.

Drew: You mean Tom?

Crystal: I never said that.

Drew: It's cute that you like him. And I'm sure he wouldn't mind. I mean, you have to accept that he's straight.

Crystal: (Chuckling under her breathe) As straight as a rainbow. Forget it; I'm not wasting my time having a heart to heart with you.

Drew: Look, whether you accept my apology or not, you should know that... (Pause) Oh god, I don't know how to explain it.

Crystal: What?

Drew: Uhhhh (long pause) …

138

DREW'S NOTEBOOK

If you can't say it try writing it, it helps

Do you want to know that bad?

It's not that. I thought this could really help you vent it out if you felt you needed to but didn't know how. Whether you tell more or not is your decision.

I do want to say it. But it's so hard to admit, even in writing.

All you have to do is start, and it'll flow from there. It's okay, take your time.

I was bullied a lot before I met you. It eventually led to a bad experience with an older boy when I was still in middle school. I hope I don't need to explain any further.

It's okay; you don't.

Take this tool with you; there is a lot of power in writing. Don't let him have any power over you anymore.

I remember right before I started middle school, my parents were worried about me having problems with other kids. I wasn't good at making friends because I thought everyone else was mean. I liked keeping to myself. I remember learning about what boys and girls are supposed to like, so I guess that's why I like sports. But I still kept to myself at recess, and usually the rest of the time. That didn't really change when middle school started. But it wasn't as easy.

From the first week of 6th grade, a group of boys I didn't even know would always be laughing and whispering when they saw me. As stupid as it was it soon escalated to taking stuff from me, like my wallet or keys, throwing food at me, spitting at me. And that escalated to being tripped in the hallway, dragged across the schoolyard by my clothes, jumped on my way home from school. Even though it was a group of boys, there was one ringleader, the rest would just hover around and laugh or do whatever he told them to. There would be times when he'd be hitting me, pushing me, dragging me, whatever involved physical contact, that his hands would take their time to let go of me, and that escalated to him feeling me up. But once his hands started to move to places they shouldn't, I stepped up.

"Get off of me!" I yelled, pushing him off of me. "What's your problem, homo?" once I said this, I could see all their jaws drop. Some of the bystanders started laughing. But he looked angry. I walked away, feeling as if I won. But on my way home from school that day, I'd come to find out how much I'd regret standing up for myself the way I did. On the same walk home I usually go through, the same one those boys would come out of nowhere and attack. This time it was the ringleader, and him alone.

I refuse to even write about it any further. I can't keep giving him power by thinking about it over and over.

After it happened, I was silent from then on. I didn't talk in school, not at home, not at all. Surprisingly I never saw him or his friends again. I didn't question it, nor did I care, I just figured they moved on to high school, maybe even dropped out. I was glad that they were gone, and I had no physical reminder of what happened. But the anger and embarrassment of being a victim remained. And then when 8th grade came, word spread of a weird nerd named Ethan who everyone thought was gay. One day in the hallway when I saw him, I made him remember me. I would scream slurs at him, then kick him from behind in the hallway. It felt good to make someone else a victim. To put myself in a more powerful position. But it was the worst thing I ever did. I let the worst thing that ever happened to me turn me into the worst possible person I could be. I constantly looked at myself as a victim, but I need to start using that pain to grow from it and become a better person because it's not too late for that.

CRYSTAL'S PHONE

April 1st

1:50 PM

Drew: Hey Crystal, it's Drew.

Crystal: Oh, hey! How'd you get my number?

Drew: Turns out I just had it. I must've got it from Anna a while ago.
Drew: I wanted to say thank you, the writing thing really helped.

Crystal: You're so welcome, I'm glad to hear it!

Drew: It made me do a lot of thinking. I know I already apologized for everything, but I know a simple I'm sorry wouldn't be enough. I really hope you can forgive me.

Crystal: I already have.

Drew: How do you do it?

Crystal: What do you mean?

Drew: Despite all the awful things I've done, you not only forgive me, but you've helped me come to terms with my own past. As happy and grateful I am, it's still something I can't manage to make sense of. At least for myself. I've never been the best at letting things go.

> Crystal: I believe in change. And your apology is genuine. Why would I dismiss it?

Drew: I'm just not proud of myself. I felt like a victim my whole life since that day, and I tried to make someone else feel the same way to make myself feel better.

> Crystal: I've obviously never experienced what you experienced, so I can't pretend that I understand what you go through. But you might be able to help someone else one day.

Drew: You really think so?

> Crystal: I know so.

Drew: Thanks. If I can ask something else, I bullied you because I wanted to pass on that feeling of being a victim to someone else. Would you ever pass that on to someone else?

> Crystal: I drag Maria on a daily basis, I don't know if that counts.
> Crystal: Honestly, I'm not like that. I just handle it differently.

Drew: I wish I could be as tough as you.

Crystal: You're not the first person to tell me that. And truthfully, I'm not as tough as you may think. I have just as many insecurities as everyone else, but I know that's just part of life.

Drew: You really are an incredible and strong person.

Crystal: Ugh I know, right?
Crystal: Thank you for helping me become that.

Drew: Thank you for showing me how easy forgiveness really is.

Crystal: Of course! I have to go. I'm working my campaign for GSA president.

Drew: Oh, you would do so good at that!

Crystal: I hope so...

May 2nd

8:15 AM

Crystal: Hey.

Maria: Hey! What's up?

Crystal: I have a really important question to ask you.

Maria: Sure, what is it?

Crystal: For the GSA campaign, you need to have a
vice president if you're running.
Crystal: If I win, do wanna be my vice president?

Maria: OMG, Crystal, are you serious?

Crystal: No, I'm kidding.
Crystal: You dork, of course, I'm serious! Who else
would I want to run GSA with me?

Maria: OMG, I love you, thank you so much! I can't
believe I'm gonna be GSA Vice President!!

Crystal: That is if I win.

Maria: Oh, come on, you really don't think you're
gonna win?

Crystal: I don't know for sure.

147

Maria: Who's your competition? Gus? Suzy?

Crystal: I don't wanna get my hopes up.

Maria: But on Thursday when you give your speech, you better walk in thinking you already won.

Crystal: Oh yeah...
Crystal: My speech...

Maria: CRYSTAL!

Crystal: Don't be mad at me; it's hard.

Maria: Dude, you're a writer, just put whatever you feel on paper.

Crystal: See this is why I need to run GSA with you.

Maria: Yeah, you're a mess without me.

Crystal: I could always get Drew to be my vice president.

Maria: That is the meanest thing you've ever said to me.

Crystal: I'll see you tomorrow, love you, loser.

Maria: Goodnight future GSA president <3

May 4th

2:51 PM

Jackie: Hey guys! You ready for tomorrow?

Suzy: I sure am!

Gus: I am! And Luke's gonna be my vice president.

Luke: I am?

Gus: You sure are <3

Maria: 2 weeks from now is the last meeting, right?

Jackie: Yep!

Suzy: How does it feel handing down the position?

Jackie: I mean I knew going into it I was only gonna have one year. It's been surreal, I've wanted to do it ever since I was a freshman, so to graduate saying I was president of the Gay-Straight Alliance is such a rewarding feeling.

Gus: How do you want to see this legacy be carried on next year?

Jackie: The position requires knowledge about the LGBTQ community and a passion to share it. You need to be open-minded, patient, and relatable. Most of all, I wanna see the next president do something that shows they won't hold back when it comes to showing their pride.

Suzy: So inspirational!!

Luke: Suck up

Maria: Leave her alone, Luke.

Gus: I love how Crystal's also running for president and isn't even active in the chat.

Crystal: I'm perfecting my speech, so I suggest you do the same if you wanna stand a chance tomorrow <3

Maria: Good luck Gus <3

GSA President Speech

I remember first hearing about the Gay-Straight Alliance as a freshman. I was frequently asked if I was a part of it because everyone seemed to assume that the little fem boy would, of course, join the GSA.

I can admit when I started high school I had a different view of the gay community. Although I knew deep in my heart that I was a part of it, I was continuously told it's not something I should be proud of. But it's finally deciding to check out the GSA for myself that made me realize that I should be proud.

The first meeting I went to, I met so many other queer students, and I realized how much I related to them. I met students who came from different cultures, different homes, but still managed to have the same hopes, fears, and dreams. They taught me that Pride is so much more than a rainbow flag. Pride is about being unapologetically your most authentic self no matter who it pisses off. Pride is about honoring the legacy that queer trailblazers of the past left behind so we can have that rainbow flag today.

I deserve to be the next GSA President because I know what it's like to feel like a lost gay fish in a sea of straights. I do not relate to LGBTQ students, I am an LGBTQ student, and I give you my word I will use this position to not only spread the message of gay pride but to spread the message that this club really stands for. Equality.

I plan to show that queer students are just as valid and worthy as any other student because at the end of the day we are the same. That is the lesson that this organization has taught me, and that is the lesson I hope to pass on. I know it is my responsibility to inspire the next generation of queer students as those before me have inspired me.

Thank you.

CRYSTAL'S PHONE

May 19th

4:52 PM

Jackie: Congratulations again your win, Crystal. I'm so happy for you!!

Crystal: Thank you so much, Jackie! I'm so excited for next year!

Jackie: Better start getting ready now.

Crystal: Please, I've been getting ready since freshman year.

Jackie: Lol, I thought so.

Crystal: I'm so proud of you, you did an amazing job this year.
Crystal: Seriously, you've been an inspiration to me since I started going to GSA. If it wasn't for you, there's no way I'd have the will to fight for this the way I did.

Jackie: Crystal, that means so much, thank you <3

Crystal: Of course! Thank you for being an example of how the GSA President should be.
Crystal: Now that it's official is there anything else I should know?

153

Jackie: It's a lot of responsibility and a lot of pressure. Week after week, queer students who are sitting where you were 2 or 3 years ago will be looking up to you as a role model and as a beacon of hope. It's so much more than just being a president of a school organization. You're gonna become a symbol of what it means to be an LGBTQ student, and you have to show how amazing and beautiful that really is, despite the bullying and discrimination. It's a lot, there's no question about that, but you won it because we all believe you have what it takes to do it.

Jackie: It's also important to remember that the next president after you could be any one of those faces in the crowd. It's your job to inspire them enough to carry on the legacy that you create.

Crystal: Thank you. For everything. From being an inspiration to being a friend and a confidant. I promise I won't let you down.

Jackie: I know you won't.
Jackie: Congratulations, and good luck <3

June 15th

4:40 PM

Crystal: Hey, Tom!
Crystal: Sorry, I know it's been a while since we've talked.
Crystal: How did your SAT go?
Crystal: Are you excited for next year?
Read

June 30th

2:30 PM

Crystal: Hey!
Crystal: We're officially seniors now!
Crystal: You there?
Read

July 20th

1:25 PM

Crystal: Hey.
Crystal: How is everything?
Crystal: How's your summer going?
Read

August 1st

4:57 PM

Tom: Hey! I heard about GSA. That's so awesome, congratulations!
Tom: How've you been?
Read

August 12th

12:38 PM

Tom: Hey.
Tom: What's up?
Tom: Sorry I wasn't able to answer any of your texts
Read

August 30th

2:55 PM

Tom: Hey.
Tom: Look, I'm sorry about everything.
Tom: You there?
Read

September 1st

10:30 AM

Maria: Hey, did I leave my charger at your house yesterday?
Maria: Hello??

Crystal: No.

Maria: Are you okay? You seemed like something was on your mind yesterday.

Crystal: I don't wanna start thinking about it again.

Maria: That's fair.
Maria: What did we agree about yesterday? How much are we putting in to buy art supplies for the GSA bulletin board?

Crystal: Honestly, that's something I've been stressing about. I don't know if I'll be able to afford everything for GSA throughout the next year.

Maria: You know what's a good idea when you're financially stressed?

Crystal: What?

Maria: Get a job.

Crystal: Now that school's coming up, I'll either be at school, doing homework, or doing chores. Besides, Tracy basically pays me to clean, so in a way, I have a job.

Maria: You're also drawing, listening to music, or watching TV, most of the time, you could totally fit a job in your schedule.

Crystal: Who's gonna be hiring during back to school season?

Maria: The mall. They're gonna start hiring early for holiday season.

Crystal: Where would I work in the mall?

Maria: There's a new dress shop opening up.

Crystal: But would they really hire someone like me?

Maria: Crystal, no, shut up.
Maria: Don't be the first one to say you can't do something because you're different. If you do, how could you expect others to not do the same?

Crystal: I can try.

Maria: You sure can.

Date: September 1ˢᵗ

Tell us a bit about yourself.
My name is Crystal, and I'm going into my senior year of high school. I am an overall A and B student, and I've been involved in my school's Gay-Straight Alliance since freshman year. During my last year of high school, I'll be president of the GSA and will have the opportunity to help LGBTQ students feel safe and included in school.

What makes you want to work for us?
I've had an interest in fashion from a very young age. Getting the opportunity to work at a dress boutique would be perfect for me since it's something I've always been so fascinated by.

How would you describe your fashion sense?
I would say my fashion sense is very broad. I can sport a punk look one day, then a softer and more feminine look the next. If I were to describe my fashion sense in one word, I'd call it unique, because it's my own.

Do you have any previous work experience?
No, I do not.

Do you have experience in fashion or as a stylist?
I've helped my friends in school with their outfits before.

What sets you apart from everyone else?

There is an obvious factor that seems to set me apart from those around me. I'm trans. Basically, I believe your body should not determine how you express yourself, whether that's how you dress or how you act. You have the power to determine that yourself. It may be something that seems to make me different, but that doesn't mean it's a problem. I'm overall grateful to have lived this life because I've been educated about a beautiful community and culture and now have a platform to teach younger students about it. And I'm proud to put it on my job application because it's something people should be more openly proud of.

What is something you've struggled with, and how did you grow past it?

Because of the way I express myself, I've unfortunately been a victim of bullying at school in the past. When I started to become more androgynous in my appearance, the bullying went from in my face to behind my back, so it became easier to ignore. But because of it, I felt depressed at an early age, and I started dealing with self-harm and suicidal ideation. But when I discovered how to express my negative feelings through hobbies like drawing or listening to music, and eventually playing with fashion and treating my wardrobe and body like it's its own art exhibit, that's when I started feeling better about myself and it became easier to remember the only person whose opinion of me matters is my own.

Describe yourself in 3 words.

Bold. Confident. Determined.

How could you benefit our shop if you get hired?

Although I don't have previous work experience, I've always been a hard worker, at school, as well as maintaining a household since my stepmother is unable to. I've always been very determined when there's something I want I do what I have to do to get it, and I take it very seriously. Combining my determination with my love of fashion will result in me doing whatever task or job I am given to the best of my ability, to satisfy myself and those around me. I'll be sure to only spread positivity in what should be an oasis for people looking for the perfect outfit for a special occasion. I am also someone who loves helping those who need it, and hopefully, leave a lasting impression, so they want to come back. I promise to live up to the expectations I am expected to meet. And that I why I know I can positively impact this store if I am lucky enough to be hired.

CRYSTAL'S PHONE

September 6th

8:22 PM

> Crystal: Maria.
> Crystal: I got it.

Maria: Got what?

> Crystal: The job.
> Crystal: They hired me.

Maria: SHUT UP!

> Crystal: I WILL NOT!
> Crystal: I met with the manager, she says she really admires my confidence and that I'd make a great addition to the staff.

Maria: OMG
Maria: THIS IS EVERYTHING
Maria: When do you start??

Crystal: Next weekend, so I'll have a feel of my school schedule by then. I just hope I can juggle everything.

Maria: Juggle what? It's your senior year; it's a walk in the park compared to our previous years. The only thing you really need to juggle a job with is GSA, but that's only one day out of each week.

Crystal: True, and I already told them I can't work Thursdays. Besides that, I'll be working some days after school as well as weekends.

Maria: Good, good.
Maria: Did you email the English teacher who advises GSA yet?

Crystal: No, thank you for reminding me. If anything, we'll see him tomorrow

Maria: Along with everyone else I've been trying all summer not to think about.

Crystal: Valid, but this is the year I'm trying to focus on what's important. Me, my grades, and GSA.

September 22nd

4:18 PM

Suzy: Today went so good! I can't believe there were so many members today.

Gus: Most of them were freshmen.

Luke: You guys were amazing as presidents, you two were so open and relatable with all of the new members. Everyone in the room had a smile on their face.

Maria: Thank you guys so much!

Crystal: Thank you guys, it means a lot. We couldn't have done it without you.

Maria: Today we had a total of 52 attendees, that's insane!

Gus: I'm pretty sure that's the biggest meeting in GSA history.

Luke: Oh, it has to be.

Suzy: Crystal, how are you feeling?

Crystal: Overall, I feel good. Today was honestly a lot easier than I thought it would be. It just came naturally.

Gus: You did okay, I guess.

Crystal: We all know today was only the beginning.
But we've experienced enough in this group to know
what to do.

Luke: You're right.

Suzy: This year's gonna be the best one yet!

September 22nd

5:03 PM

Drew: Hey! How did GSA go? Sorry I couldn't be there.

Crystal: Hey, It was good! And you're fine; there was more than enough people that came, way more than what Maria and I expected anyway.

Drew: How many people were there?

Crystal: 52

Drew: Crystal, that's amazing!

Crystal: Thanks, Drew. It's definitely gonna be a lot of names to remember.

Drew: Do you think it'll be that many every week?

Crystal: Honestly, I'd hope not.

Drew: Really, why?

Crystal: It was overwhelming, to be honest. I still got through it, according to the council members I did a good job. But it was a lot of pressure.

Drew: That's understandable, but you'll get used to it as time goes on.

Crystal: You think so?

Drew: Totally. You know how strong you are.
Drew: With this platform, you have an opportunity to change our school and really leave your mark. I'm so excited for you.

Crystal: The last time a football player was this nice to me was... well, that was an experience.

Drew: I think we're both agreed we won't let that happen to you again.

Crystal: I'd appreciate it.
Crystal: Have you talked to him at all?

Drew: Who? Tom?

Crystal: Yeah. I've tried to reach out, but he's never responded.

Drew: I never bothered; he was never my biggest fan anyway. Besides, I'm probably the last person he'd wanna hear from.
Drew: What about Anna?

Crystal: You think I've bothered?

Crystal: Why do you ask about her after what she did to you? I know you're all about forgiveness now, but she's done a lot of unforgivable stuff, especially to you.

Drew: You forgave me, didn't you?

Crystal: That's different.

Drew: How so?
Drew: After what I've been through, and how I've learned to right my wrongs, I believe she can do the same thing.

Crystal: I hope so.

Act 2 Scene 4: School Hallway

(Lights go on. The next day, Drew approaches Tom)

Drew: Hey

Tom: What do you want?

Drew: (almost ashamed) I realize how ridiculous my behavior's been, and I'm really sorry, Tom.

Tom: You're apologizing to the wrong person; go talk to Crystal.

Drew: I did already did, but I wanted to talk to you.

Tom: Drew, you tried to make a beautiful girl feel insecure and small, and for what? Just because she's different?

Drew: (Getting the wind kicked out of himself) Yeah, I had my own shit going on... I wanna be an ally...

Tom: An ally? —Here's something just for you then... I like guys (pause) I like girls. I like people

Drew: (smiling) Good for you.

(They shake hands. Lights dim)

ANNA'S PHONE

October 14th

7:32 AM

Tracy: Have you been going to school? Are you going today??

Anna: It's a Saturday, you psycho.

Tracy: No, it's Friday.
Tracy: Look, if you don't want to come home, fine, but at least get your education.

Anna: Why is that the most important thing in the world to you? You know it takes more than just nagging your kid about their schoolwork to be a good parent. What, did you miss the love and nurture lesson at parenting school?

Tracy: I get it, I've made mistakes, but look where we live, look what we have now. Why would you want to give that up?

Anna: I don't care if it's a mansion, I can't call it home if you sleep right across the hall from me.

Tracy: Why are so hateful?

Anna: Look at the example I had growing up.

170

Tracy: No one is perfect. Why can't parents make mistakes too?

Anna: The fights you had with dad, right in front of me, as violent and scary as they'd get, that was just a mistake?

Anna: Refusing to say I Love You out in public because you didn't want to look weak was just a mistake?

Anna: Flat out neglecting all parenting responsibilities, then rubbing it in my face that I should be grateful because you got lucky and married well, just a mistake?

Tracy: At the end of the day, you can either continue to blame me for what you turned out to be or take responsibility for it and do what you can to change it. I know I messed up, multiple times, but you're nearly a grown woman. You have the power to change the direction of your life now.

Anna: Now you wanna try to act all wise?

Tracy: I've always been, you just don't care to notice when I do something right.

Anna: If you hate the way I am, so much enjoy taking it up with the person that raised me for the rest of your life.

"You should really shave if you're trying to look feminine, you don't want to make anybody uncomfortable" "The way you present yourself is unprofessional and offensive" "That's not sexual assault, he only touched your chest" "But didn't you sleep with him anyway?"

I'll never understand why a parent would raise their child to fear the outside world. I'll never understand why a parent would lead their child to believe they're hated, toxic, and broken. I'll never understand why a parent would invalidate every thought, every opinion, every word that their child has to share. I'll never understand why a parent would try to embarrass and ridicule their child in front of others. I'll never understand why my Wicked Stepmother always asserted dominance over me as if motherhood was more a position of power than of care and love

I'm not perfect. I've made more mistakes than I can count. Throughout your life, my negative perception of myself pushed me to say a lot of hurtful things to you. And I truly believed I could make up for it through money. I look at it now as if it's in the past. Now, I love you more than words can say. I want nothing more than to take away every mean thing I've ever said to you. You are a symbol of my biggest dream come true. To become a mother. But as you've reminded me time and time again, you are also a symbol of all of my bad actions. Truthfully, I believed you to be a lot stronger. I thought my words wouldn't bother you the way they did. If it means anything now, you're not worthless; you're not a waste of space, you're not a failure. You're beautiful, smart, and determined. If my words have power, then please let those kind words mean as much as the bad words did. I want to fix this between us because I know it's my fault.

But first and foremost I want you to be happy, and I want to go by whatever you want. There's no excuse for what I did. But hopefully, you'll have a better understanding of what my position is like when you have your own child. If the distance between us will bring that to you, then I'll do whatever needs to be done. I know time will heal both of our wounds.

I know it's not easy to believe, but I have given my best efforts to be a proper mother for you. But it doesn't matter if it was my best because I still didn't do a good job. I'm no fool; I know what your ultimate opinion of me is. You have every right to feel whatever you want to feel. And at the end of the day, that's your truth. But I didn't see it that way. I couldn't be any more sorry for my conservative remarks in the past and my inability to accept what I didn't fully understand. Growing up on this island, you're taught only to accept one kind of person. But you've proven that what deviates from the norm is just as beautiful and worthy. You make me so proud. No matter what you choose, all I hope for is your happiness.

Love Mom

DREW'S PHONE

December 15th

4:01 PM

Shay: OMG! Drew! What's going on with Anna? Are her and Ethan really stepsiblings?

Drew: You know her name is Crystal, right?
Drew: And Anna's been back and forth ever since what happened with Crystal and Tom

Shay: What do you mean? What happened with Ethan and Tom?
Shay: Or Crystal, whatever it is.

Drew: Oh, I thought everyone knew at this point.
Drew: Anna snuck into the ball where Crystal and Tom kissed, she had me come with her and blackmailed me into reading a personal note Crystal had written about Tom on a loudspeaker.

Shay: No way

Drew: I'm only telling you because I know you and Anna are close. Don't say anything.

Shay: Of course.

THE CHEERLEADERS GROUP CHAT

December 15th

4:10 PM

Shay: YOU GUYS!!
Shay: YOU WILL NOT BELIEVE WHAT I JUST FOUND OUT!

Steph: OMG, what?

Erika: This seems so important.

Shay: That whole thing about Tom hooking up with Ethan, Tom never bragged about it, Anna made that up.
Shay: And get this. Ethan is Anna's stepbrother!

Didi: No way.

Shay: Way.
Shay: And also, Anna snuck into the party where they kissed and blackmailed Drew into reading something embarrassing that Ethan wrote on a loudspeaker or something.

Erika: Why would she do something like that?

Shay: I don't know, Drew told me, so I guess it's true.

Steph: Valid.

176

Didi: Omg, poor Crystal, I can't believe Anna would do that to her own stepbrother.

Erika: You mean, Ethan?

Shay: His name is Ethan, but he calls himself Crystal

Didi: Ohhhh.

Steph: I wonder if anyone else knows.

Erika: Oh, I already texted all my guy friends about it. They didn't know anything, but they do now.

Steph: Who else should we tell?

Shay: The word will spread soon enough...

CRYSTAL'S PHONE

December 17th

7:45 PM

Anna: Are you the one that started spreading that crap about me?

Crystal: I am not, and what do you mean crap? It's all true.

Anna: Who hate's me this much to spread rumors about me?

Crystal: It sucks doesn't it.

Anna: You're just loving every second of this, aren't you?

Crystal: I find it funny. Everyone's acting sympathetic toward me now, not realizing that it was months ago and we're all over it. But leave it to high school to bring back the drama you want to forget.

Anna: And everyone wonders why we hate it.

Crystal: It's a big school — one of the biggest in the state. Everyone's competing with one another. And they'll do whatever they can to bury others to get to the top.

Anna: You can just say you're talking about me.

Crystal: Do I need to? You figured it out.

Anna: I'm sorry. For everything. I get it now. You deserve a lot more respect then you get.
Anna: Crystal?

Crystal: Do you really get what it's like now?

Anna: I'll never be able to fully understand. But I can, a little bit now.
Anna: So, how are you enjoying everyone feeling sorry for you now?

Crystal: It's been fun, for sure.
Crystal: What about you? How does it feel to be the Most Popular Freak in School?

Anna: How did it feel for you?

Crystal: Fabulous.

My Ugly Stepsister

When I say the word ugly, I don't mean how you look. The words ugly and beauty are so much more than appearance. But when you forget that is when the ugly in you shows. You're someone else who's appeared to me in many different forms throughout my life. You're my real stepsiblings, in times where they've put me in a place where I'm stuck feeling less than, in a household where age means worth, and acts of kindness are out of pity. You are every bully I've known, in person, or hiding behind a keyboard. You are every "Faggot!" You are every "Freak!" You are every "You're Worthless!" You are every "Go Kill Yourself!"

More than anything, you have become self-doubt, every "I'm not good enough" every insult I say in my head to myself, every time I look in the mirror and am appalled by what I see. You are every bout of anxiety, every paranoid thought. You are the voice in my head trying to convince me that everyone around me hates me, that I make everyone I know uncomfortable. You are the distorted self-image that remains from the years of being put in a box of ridicule and pain. But I've experienced the worst already. I thought I've already faced my Ugly Stepsister and won. But you just won't go away. Your power needs to be taken away. You don't get to be the reason why I should have to be protected from myself.

You no longer have the power to look down on me. You have no place telling me I'm not good enough. You are no longer allowed to fill my head with self-deprecating thoughts,.

My Ugly Stepsister, I'm letting you go, and I will only convert the negativity you filled me with into positive energy. That's how I plan to use my disadvantage to my advantage

Love is so many things. Love can be romance, roses, and all the stereotypical, expected bullshit. Love is also with family and all of those who are closest to you. I Love my family. I Love my friends. I Love my dogs. I Love my bed.

Love is also different for everyone. Some people don't feel love as strong as others do. Some claim they don't feel love at all. I've always felt like a very loving person. And sometimes, if not most of the time, I'm not too good at showing it. And it bothers me because I want the ones that I love to feel it, not just know it. It's taken a long time for me to be able to easily show love and care.

I've broken more than one heart. The first I think of is one of my best friends from 7th grade to 10th grade. In 10th grade is when we finally admitted we liked each other. Even when I started wearing makeup, she stayed supportive. Even when I still loved someone toxic and cold, she stayed supportive. But as I got happier, she got sadder, and I felt her dragging me down. So I broke it off. I tried to be a friend to her still. But I hurt her. I hurt a lot of people. And I feel guilty. For a while, I felt alone. I stopped loving myself. High school really fucks you up like that. And now as an adult, I'm just expected to be okay. It's hard, but I'm doing it. No one's perfect. I Love Myself.

I Love Myself. I Love Myself. I Love Myself. I Love Myself. I Love Myself. I Love Myself. I Love Myself. I Love Myself. I Love Myself.

Dear Prince Charming

For someone I've never really gotten to know, you've been able to heavily affect my life, the way I think, and the way I act. In the past, you've determined where I go, how long I stay, what I get involved in. You've clouded my judgment, and you've distracted me from what was more important. You've appeared to me at school, in the hallways or in classrooms. You appear to me from day to day when I'm walking, when I'm commuting. You've appeared to me through my phone and through social media. And most often throughout my life, for as long as I can remember, you've appeared to me through film, TV shows, and books. No matter how universal you really are, you've made me feel like there was a real personal connection between just us. But every time I conclude that you're nothing more than an imaginary figure full of idealistic delusion.

Although you have the power to appear to disillusioned young girls, and boys, as a human figure, fitting their visual idealization of a knight in shining armor, you're not a real person at all. You are an idea. You are a concept. You are ultimately something that isn't real but can still exist in someone's own personal reality. What's crazier is how everyone seems to have their own image of what you really look like. To me, you've always been tall, rather muscular, dark haired. Maybe some tattoos and piercings. I've always pictured you as very masculine and domineering, but caring and affectionate at the same time. You've appeared to me before through people I've met. Or at least I've thought you did. I've come across many little boys trying to meet the expected standards of what it means to be a Prince Charming. But every time the guise of a perfect savior is diminished by a broken personality and a whole mess of toxic masculinity. I guess Prince Charming isn't just an image little girls and boys have of their knight in shining armor coming to save them with love, but it's also an image to little boys of what they should grow up to become. But the idea of a Prince Charming is impossible because perfection is impossible.

Over the years, I've picked many, many, MANY men that match or at least come close to matching the physical appearance of my ideal Prince Charming. And even though they all look different, I always convince myself they possess the same ideal personality that my Prince Charming has, even though it's never the case. I've always imagined you were too perfect to have your own problems. But everyone has their own struggles, even Prince Charming.

Whether you're real or not, you still exist in my reality, whether I like it or not. I just gave up looking so hard for you. So I've decided, if you are real, it's time I chill, live my life, and let you come to me in whatever form you choose to come in, because you may not be the image I've carried throughout my life. I've always wanted a Prince Charming, but I've always needed a companion, and that doesn't have to be a savior like you. I'll always keep my eye out for you, but not having something is not worth the heartbreak when I already have so much to keep my heart whole.

The most memorable time I came across you was when I did my first play, and I was the princess, and the actor next to me was playing Prince Charming. Despite his portrayal of such a perfect and likable man, it wasn't real. He used his charm to manipulate and fool those around him, including me, as most Prince Charming's do. That only proved to me that you're not real, and people playing the part of the Prince Charming can often turn out to become the villain. I've always felt indifferent towards you, but at the end of the day, all that heartbreak you threw my way made me stronger. Thanks for that, I guess.

I remember my grandmother was there for me more than anyone else. I remember her house. I remember her tomato garden. I remember the markers and crayons and drawing books she got for me. I remember the stories we made up together. I remember feeling like she was the last person I had to celebrate my creativity with. I remember still feeling like a burden to her whenever she got fed up or wanted to be alone. I remember the last time I saw her in the hospital, totally unaware of what was to come. I remember wishing I knew I wasn't gonna see her again. I remember the last time I saw her smile.

Act 2 Scene 6: Cemetery

(Maria and Tom enter a vacant area of the cemetery, away from the tombstones, and Crystal, presenting as Ethan, is alone by a tree.)

Tom: I'm confused. Why would you bring me out to an old cemetery?

Maria: Because I knew this is where Crystal would be.

(As Tom approaches Crystal, Maria plays spectator from behind.)

Tom: Crystal? Is that you?

Crystal: (Turns around, first shocked to see him, then embarrassed, she gets up, and tries to leave.) You shouldn't be here.

Tom: I'm sorry. This is really you?

Crystal: The real me. So happy you get to see it finally.

186

Tom: Crystal, are you okay?

Crystal: As if you care. Anna showed me what you said. I'm clingy, annoying, embarrassing. I'm a freak

Tom: You really believe I said those horrible things?

Crystal: I don't know Tom! Everyone has been playing with my feelings, and I'm really sick of it.

Tom: Crystal, I get you're upset, but you're acting a bit melodramatic right now.

Crystal: What exactly were you trying to do? What, you just thought you could come in and sweep me off my feet and be my knight in shining armor?

Tom: Are you even being authentic, or are you just trying to be overdramatic?

Maria: (Trying to get between Tom and Crystal) Okay... We have a lot of tension between us right now, so let's calm down, take a deep breath, and...

Crystal: (Interrupts Maria, and pushes her out of the way) Now I'm overdramatic?

Tom: Yeah. For a while, you've acted like everything about your life sucks. Some people have it worse than you because you have a support system. Me, Maria, GSA. Some people don't have that luxury. You can't focus on the negative you need to stay positive. I've tried to be your friend, but this is too much to handle. Maybe freak isn't the right term, maybe bitch is.

(Crystal slaps Tom.)

Crystal: I don't need to be reprimanded or insulted by someone like you.

Tom: You think you know me so well don't you?

Crystal: (angry) I've known dozens of yous!

Maria: (Steps back in) All right, that's enough. You two are friends. Just shake hands and makeup

Tom: Forget it, I got to go (Exits with all the wind knocked out of his heart.)

Maria: (To Crystal) Do you really think all that stuff Anna said is true?

Crystal: Isn't everyone the same in the end?

Maria: Can you ever think normally? First, you were blinded by love, and now you're blinded by anger and hate

Crystal: I was blinded by love, now I see perfectly fine. People play with hearts like they're toys. But the main problem was being forced to act like a boy. Tracy would get so mad at me over everything! My dad was the only one who let me shop in the girl's section.

(Maria moves closer to Crystal and tries to console her.)

But the one thing I wanted just as much I wanted to be free of this body was someone to hold me and protect me from all the hate in the world and to wipe away my tears and tell me that everything's going to be okay. Everyone always told me, "you're so confident, you're so brave," but I'm not. I'm terrified.

Maria: I hope you know you are a beautiful strong and outgoing person. You just need to let yourself be happy.

Crystal: I've been threatened, harassed, stared at wherever I go, and as much as I pretend it doesn't bother me, it does. It hurts knowing how judgmental people are. And I wanted somebody who I love, and who loves me to be there for me but no. No one loves someone who's different. People like me don't get happy endings…

One day, towards the end of my senior year of high school, I was texting a friend I had just seen that day about a friend of hers. I was sitting with a boy in the backseat of a car when I was with her and another friend. A boy who I'd known since middle school, who I haven't seen in a long time until that point. He was really cute, and always had been. At one point we were good friends, but when I was with him, he did nothing but look the other way. I texted the girl that was there and asked her if he didn't like me. She told me it was quite the opposite and that he actually had a crush on me. I was surprised but happy, mostly because I thought he didn't like me at all. She told me he was meeting her at the park later and told me to go in her place. I met him near the train station, we walked to the park, and I tried to catch up with him since this was the first day, we've seen each other in so long. He said he was tired and might not stay for long. Before he left, I told him what I was told, that he was attracted to me. He was angry, but not at me. He said he was angry because she was lying. He was someone who struggled with his sexuality in the past, and he said it was something she constantly brought back up. I called that same girl, and she continued to say he liked me and that he was denying it. We walked back to the train, and I wanted to make sure it ended on good terms. He told me if he really liked me, he'd make it obvious. She told me he was a dick, and I deserved better. I never found out what really happened. But the two alternatives appeared as either it was too embarrassing for someone to admit they were attracted to me, or I was used as a tool to embarrass somebody, which ultimately only makes me look like the joke in the end. Nothing but something stupid that happened in high school at the end of the day, but it's a shitty feeling being trapped in the dark only knowing that you're being made fun of, and not exactly knowing what's happening on the other end.

The summer after I graduated high school before I started college, I started talking to a photographer I knew from high school about my play, because I knew I might want a photographer to help promote it. Days later, I heard from him again, talking about his sexuality and resulted in a day-long conversation full of flirting and ended with a plan to meet the next day. It took a long time for us to actually meet since he was so back and forth with whether or not he actually wanted to talk to me. By the end of it, it turned out he was gay, and I was only second best when he got a boyfriend. This time there weren't really any questions, I was used as a tool to figure out his sexuality.

Maybe now it's easier to understand why Crystal couldn't entirely trust Tom. Incidents like these left me thinking, "What's wrong with me?" Almost every interaction I had felt like an embarrassing incident, and I constantly felt in the dark, unaware of the jokes and insults that were being shared behind my back. Such was the life of a queer person, but no one is ever really alone, and sometimes it takes a last resort to bounce back.

Act 2 Scene 7: Crystal's House

(Lights go on. Tracy's talking on the phone, and Crystal comes in, as Ethan)

Crystal: Tracy, can we talk?

Tracy: (To Crystal) I know you see me talking on the phone! (To phone) Anyway...

Crystal: (Takes the phone from Tracy, hangs it up, and puts it down.) Mom, we need to talk.

Tracy: Ugh fine. What is it?

Crystal: Well, it all started when I caught feelings for my friend.

Tracy: Do I know her? It's Maria, isn't it?

Crystal: No, his name is Tom. But I'm not gay.

Tracy: Are you one of those bisexuals?

Crystal: Can you just listen?

Tracy: I don't have time for this (starts to walk away)

Crystal: Sure, ignore me like always

Tracy: (stops, faces Crystal) Do you think it's easy for me? I hate the thought of you being upset or hurt that's why I run from it, or get mad or push you away and you know what... I was never able to do it on my own. I'll never be as good as your dad was. He was always there for you. He was always there for me too. I never tell you enough, but I do love you. I'm sorry that I'm mean and disconnected at times.

(They embrace.)

Crystal: I'm not a boy.

Tracy: What?

Crystal: I'm trans. I have the mind and personality of a girl. I am a girl. I like boys; I wear makeup and girl clothes.

Tracy: That's why you and Anna fight like that!

Crystal: You're okay with this?

Tracy: Ethan, you're my son. Well, daughter. I can't reject you for being who you are. What about this boy that you like?

Crystal: Oh, he's sweet, handsome, and understanding. Overall charming. But we argued the last time we spoke.

Tracy: How do you know him?

Crystal: He's Maria's cousin

Tracy: Don't let this whole thing weigh you down, and maybe you'll get somewhere with this Tom kid. (They hug.) I Love You, Ethan.

Crystal: Actually, can you call me, Crystal?

Tracy: Crystal…(Pause) Okay.

Crystal is alone inside of a dressing room in her high school's auditorium. She was given responsibility for the costumes for the spring musical, and when she had the opportunity after rehearsals were over, she put on a yellow dress that had belonged to the lead. She's looking in the mirror adjusting the skirt when all of a sudden, the door opens and Belle, the lead, enters. Crystal turns around, shocked and embarrassed

Crystal: Belle! I'm so sorry; I didn't realize anyone else was still here…

Belle: Crystal, you look incredible!

Crystal: What?

Belle: Just the skirt's a little bunched up, I'll fix it for you

Belle adjusts the skirt and turns Crystal towards the mirror

Belle: See how much better that is?

Crystal: I'm sorry.

Belle: What are you sorry for?

Crystal: This is your dress.

Belle: It never fit me right, and it's too hard for me to walk in. You look way better in it; it's almost like it's made for you.

Crystal: You really think so?

Belle: Are you kidding? You pull it off effortlessly.

Crystal: Wow, thank you.

Belle: And you've done such a good job with all of the costumes.

Crystal: Thank you, but it's not just me, the whole art department deserves credit.

Belle: Is costume design something you want to go into?

Crystal: Just art in general, I guess.

Belle: I've always loved what the art department does for the spring musical every year. I wish I was that talented.

Crystal: You're playing the main character.

Belle: I know, but there's plenty of talented kids in this school that can act and sing. What you do is so brave, I've always looked up to you.

Crystal: Thank you so much!

Belle: What's your sign?

Crystal: Cancer.

Belle: Same! My birthday's at the end of June

Crystal: Me too!

Belle: What day?

Crystal: The 29th

Belle: You're lying.

Crystal: Do we have the same birthday?

Belle: It's like you're my long lost twin!

Crystal: Oh please, I wish I was as pretty as you.

Belle: Do you see how you look in this dress? *(turns Crystal toward the mirror again)*

Crystal: You're not wrong

The two newfound friends laugh together

Belle: I'm probably gonna head home in a bit, do you need a ride home?

Crystal: No, I'm okay, thank you, I need to clean up a little more before I head out. After I take this off anyway.

Belle: It doesn't look too bad, why don't you just save it for tomorrow?

196

Crystal: I'd prefer to get it over with. Besides, cleaning never bothered me anyway.

Belle: Alright, I'll see you, tomorrow love!

They hug before Belle exits & Crystal is left by herself.

In times where it really seemed like no one was on my side, even the littlest acts of kindness began to mean absolutely everything to me. But sometimes in such a toxic environment, it was hard to tell when kindness was real or when it wasn't...

Crystal watches as Belle walks down the hall and laughs while texting on her phone. She looks back at Crystal, still laughing, before walking off, leaving Crystal alone.

January 12th
Principal S,

I have a lot of concerns regarding a senior's involvement in this year's spring musical, which I, of course, will be directing. This student by the name of Ethan but refers to him/herself as "Crystal." This is the crossdresser I'm sure you've heard much about. You know, the one who runs that club after school for the younger gay students, oh bless his/her soul. Now, I'm concerned because this student spoke to an art teacher about being involved in the spring musical. This concerns me because I don't want to deal with having to tell him/her that (s)he won't be able to audition for female roles. Now I just want to state I have so much love and support for the transgender community. My best friend is actually transgender, and (s) he is so inspiring and beautiful. But beside the point, I do not want to break this brave, but odd individuals spirit if I have to explain that I cannot give a feminine, delicate role to someone like that. It's simply not the theatre way. I would be more than willing to offer a lesser male role to fit him/her better. I wouldn't be able to offer him/her the main role either because I simply do not want to make the audience uncomfortable. I'm sure you can understand and will hopefully be on my side if (s)he gets triggered or something. Thank you for your time, and have a blessed day.

Sincerely,
The Music Teacher

THE GSA GROUP CHAT

February 6th

2:55 PM

Gus: So, word spread about Crystal wanting a female role in the spring musical. The music teacher was talking about it.

Crystal: omg, can we stop talking about it? Did you guys forget I'm in this group chat?

Luke: How are you feeling? You can vent to us if you want.

Crystal: I asked about helping out with costumes for the spring musical, not auditioning for a role
Crystal: I just got out of the principal's office because the music teacher emailed him.

Maria: What happened?

Crystal: This is the first time I've had the opportunity to sit and talk with the principal. Everyone says he's strict, but he was actually really nice to me. He told me he respects what the GSA did and thanked me for the work we've done.

Suzy: Aw, yay!!

Maria: So, you're okay?

Crystal: Overall, yes, that put me in a very good mood.
Crystal: But a part of me is extremely infuriated that even the teachers are disrespecting me now.
Crystal: It just feels like, after everything we've done, there's no change. If I'm being treated this way, how are they gonna treat queer students next year when I'm not here anymore? It feels like trans people in this town still get put in a box when we're just people. These are kids trying to get an education, and it is not fair that something they can't even control is getting in the way, all because of people's ignorance and inability to accept others.

Luke: *applause*

Maria: Queen

Crystal: Am I not a good GSA president? Is that why nothing's changing?

Gus: After the way you just went off, you're gonna question if you're a good president or not? You got elected because of your passion to fight for a cause. And what really proves you were meant for this, you're saying you want to fix these issues for others, not you. Your selflessness is what's gonna make you thrive.

Crystal: You guys mean so much to me. All I do is complain about literally everything. But I need to be a lot more grateful. There are trans students that don't have a single friend or even a roof to sleep under. That's why this is so important to me.

Maria: You need to take that passion and use it to make a change. Be bold. Think outside the box. You're smart, and you've done it before.

Crystal: How?

Maria: Just by simply dressing the way you do in our closed-minded, conservative school, that is making waves. Do you not realize how many kids came out after you came to school in drag with your purple wig? Do you not realize how GSA flourished since you started doing what you do? You're a trailblazer. Crystal's catch light and create a rainbow, just like how you create and spread pride in the world.

Gus: And most of all, you're a queen, and a queen has the right to put peasants in their place.

Maria: Besides, this is one teacher out of how many? A lot of the faculty are very supportive of GSA

Gus: Literally all of the English teachers

Luke: The drama teachers, the gym teachers

Suzy: The art teachers!

Maria: Even the security guards want to see this club continue to flourish. We can't let a few negative voices snuff us out.

Crystal: We need to do something big. We need to show this school that queer students are here and they're not leaving anytime soon, no matter how hard you try to shut them out.

Maria: What do you have in mind?

Crystal: When is Transgender Pride Day again?

Gus: March 31st, I believe.

Crystal: We have time.

Luke: For what??

Crystal: We're gonna make a banner
Crystal: It's gonna be pink blue and white

Suzy: Ooh, fun!

Crystal: I want dozens of little trans pride flags printed out that says something like "I Support Trans Rights" or "We Support Trans Rights."

Luke: Gus and I can take care of that.

Gus: Oh, we sure can!

Maria: This is so exciting. What exactly are you planning?

Crystal: Something historic.
Crystal: But first there's definitely some peasants that I need to settle things with.

THE CHEERLEADER'S GROUP CHAT

February 17th

2:21 PM

Didi: Did you guys pay senior dues yet?

Erika: They were due by the end of January.

Didi: Oh
Didi: Yeah, I knew that.

Shay: Do you think Anna's gonna show her face at prom?

Erika: I would hope not we're already gonna have her freakshow stepbrother there.

Didi added Crystal to the chat

Shay: wtf???

Didi: Oh, she said to add her if anyone was talking about her.

Steph: Wait, so is it he or she?

Crystal: The ultimate she, don't forget it.
Crystal: I wanted to say something about the conversations that go on about me behind my back

Shay: I don't know what you're talking about.

Crystal: You know I can see the texts from before I was added, right?
Crystal: I'm not gonna continue this argument. If you choose to be close-minded toward a beautiful community and culture, that's not my problem. I hope you learn to spread some love.

Shay: I am such a supporter of the GBLT community, how could you say that?

Didi: Isn't there a Q?

Crystal: The same girls that are allies only to the pretty gay boys, I've seen laugh at me and then whisper about me to their friends when I first wore makeup and feminine clothes. You're not the best supporter of this community, and you don't need to be, your opinions are your own. By all means, if you want to spend the remainder of the "best four years of our lives" talking about me, that's fine, I love being the topic of conversation. But what we should do is not make fun of my stepsister. We're here for education after all.

Shay: You're seriously dumb enough to defend someone who tried to ruin her reputation?

Crystal: Kindness is real. Hopefully, you realize that for yourself.

Crystal left the chat

THE JOCK'S GROUP CHAT

February 21st

1:28 PM

Cole: Drew, did you go to the club with all those cringy gay kids yesterday? Bro, don't become the next Tom.

Drew: What are you talking about? GSA?

Frank: Is that what it's called?

Cole: The club hosted by the gay kid in makeup. You know what I'm talking about.

Drew: That gay kid in makeup is my friend, and I was only going to support her.

John: So, he is becoming the next Tom.

Frank: You'd really betray us the same way he did?

Drew: Betray? Really? You're so dramatic about it.

John: You really wanna turn into one of those freaks like Tom did, by all means. If there's anyone I hate more than him, it's his "girlfriend."

Drew added Crystal to the chat

Cole: Drew, wtf?

Drew: She had some things she wanted to get off her chest.

Crystal: John my love, you've been saying you hate me since I first wore lipstick to school, that was over two years ago. If you were really that passionate about it, you could've said it to my face by now.

John: Now you wanna catch an attitude you perv?

Crystal: Perv, really? Other than the way you guys look, is there really anything to like about you?

John: Most of our school wants you dead. You don't fit in. You aren't wanted. You're an abomination.

Crystal: If my alternative is being anything like you "popular" kids, I'm more than happy being an abomination. And what are any of you gonna do, block me? That's all any of you are brave enough to do anyway. None of you would lay your hands on me because there's a voice at the back of your head telling you "don't touch the gay, it's contagious." What it comes down to is none of you have the nerve you claim you have to do the things you threaten behind my back. You're cowards. And that's the tea.

John: You're the lowest of the low. You really think you can wave a rainbow flag and think everyone's gonna accept you? You aren't entitled to anything! You having rights isn't a debate, your below everyone else. This is a fight that you cannot and will not win. You're never gonna make this school or this island a safe place for yourself or any other fag.

Crystal: Challenge accepted.

Crystal left the chat

Liberation is an important word for the queer community. Liberation is an important word for the entire world. The dictionary definition for the word liberation is *a movement seeking equal rights and status for a group.* Liberation is something we've seen throughout history time after time after time. Liberation is something we should all know, remember, and hold on to. We've

seen liberation in this world when women fought for and earned their right to vote and stand equal to men in society. We saw liberation in our world when people of different races and cultures came together to stand up for their rights and equality. Liberation presented itself to us when the queer community rioted for their rights on Christopher Street in New York late June of 1969. Liberation is something that I thought I fully understood as a queer teenager who's spit in the face of ignorance and discrimination. As a young adult, I'm only honored and excited learning more and more about what it means to live authentically queer, and what it means to be liberated.

I first admitted that I liked boys when I was 13. Even then, before I even got to the topic of my gender identity, I thought I knew anything and everything I needed to know about being LGBTQ. I thought I fully knew what liberation meant when I finally admitted I liked boys after years of being called a faggot. I never fully understood why I was targeted by bullies as much as I was, whether it was my femininity, or just being a weird, nerdy kid. Feeling alone, isolated and bullied for so long can either push someone to live in fear or to live in strength. To be honest, even six years later, I still don't know which one I fell into. As humans, we live in both fear and strength. I choose to stay on the side of strength as much as possible.

In today's world, living in fear is the worst thing you can do, even if sometimes it feels like the easiest thing to do. Humanity tends to threaten what they don't understand. Humanity often picks and chooses what they include in their reality and throws everything else to the side. Humanity tends to take groups of people and socially outcast them. I've seen that the feeling of fear can fade away among queer people when they discover their community. I thought I knew what liberation was when I was president of my high schools Gay Straight Alliance. I thought I knew what liberation was when I wrote and starred in my own play about my experience as a queer high school student. I thought I knew what liberation was when I competed in my first pageant as Crystal Tyler and placed as 3rd Alternate. I thought I knew what liberation was when I was bullied. I thought I knew what liberation was when I was held naked in a doorway. I thought I knew what liberation was when I was given up on and shipped off to a psych ward. But what I've learned from all of these experiences is that this is not just my journey. My pride and my art is only a small part of an entire community experiencing pride, freedom, love, and liberation. I've always said it's important as a queer person today to carry out the legacy created by people who have lost their lives for this movement and continue to inspire the generation of queer people that comes after you to continue waving that rainbow flag, and that is all I hope to do. Liberation has a growing definition for everybody. Queer or not all we can ever do is continue to grow through education, through art, through experience, and pride.

CRYSTAL'S PHONE

March 31st

7:55 AM

Drew: Crystal.
Drew: Did you by any chance have anything to do with the big transgender pride flag hanging in the front of the school?

Crystal: Duh.

Drew: And the little flags that say "I Support Trans Rights" all over the hall?

Crystal: I can't take credit for all of it, my GSA council helped.
Crystal: How's everyone reacting?

Drew: More confused than anything. Teachers and students are either giving it an uncomfortable stare or just trying to ignore it. I don't even think some of them know what it means.

Crystal: Oh, I'm sure they do. It says "trans rights" on it.

Drew: Your name is all anyone is saying right now. I'm at the front of the school where you put the flag.
Drew: Why did you do it?

212

Crystal: The flag is a symbol. Even if you don't agree with what you see, you can still go to school, mind your business, and get your education.

Crystal: This is for the queer kids to know that despite what's put against us, they're never alone. And school IS a safe place for them.

March 31ˢᵗ
Crystal,

You're actions today were historic. You have proven you are willing to fight to give a voice to those who don't have one. You have used what some may consider a disadvantage to your advantage and brought awareness to a mainstream issue to make our school a safer and more open place, as well as giving strength to the more vulnerable. You have been an example, and a role model to your peers and that is why I am proud to present you with this year's Public Advocate Scholarship award for the work you have done for our community and the LGBTQ community.

And I'm very impressed with the work you've done in your art class. I'd love for you to design this year's Senior T-Shirt.

Congratulations and thank you for all you've done.

Sincerely,
Principal S.

Confessions of a GSA President

Unless you are a queer person, there's no possible way you can say you understand what it's like to be LGBTQ. But the beautiful thing about a Gay-Straight Alliance, or Gender Sexuality Alliance as it's been renamed at my old school, is it's a place for students of every identity to come together to celebrate equality, love, and acceptance. Especially in high school, that's a hard thing to come by. And it takes a special kind of person to facilitate that sort of atmosphere. Sadly, even though I held the position, I questioned whether or not I was a special enough kind of person. The truth was, and still is, GSA my first two years of high school, was always a place for me to be myself and talk about whatever I wanted, whatever I felt like I needed to talk about. When I became president that got taken away and replaced with responsibilities. I never got the time to step back and take it all in. And I wasn't allowed just to let loose and feel comfortable anymore. I had to maintain a certain image and become as positive and open as the group I was running. I had to embody the message I was trying to get across. I'm not saying I wasn't ready, because I accomplished some wonderful things during my reign, but it's hard running a club for queer students who need your help and guidance when you still are a queer student who needs help and guidance. Maybe I tried too hard to live up to the presidents that came before me. Perhaps I had too premature of an understanding of what being queer meant. But I did my best then, and I'm doing my best now. I held that position because I had a passion to share my pride and inspire others to do so. And I did that.

My biggest insecurities have been verbalized to me before. "No matter how hard you try, you'll never wipe out bullying. Your pride is pointless. This is not a fight worth fighting. You're outnumbered". It's hard being shot down even when you do everything you can to stand up for yourself and others. But all it takes is one voice to remind me why it's important never to stop spreading the message.

CRYSTAL'S PHONE

May 19th

2:09 PM

TJ: Hey! This is TJ. I'm a sophomore; I go to GSA. I wanted to talk to you because I'm thinking about running for president.

Crystal: Hey! You should totally go for it. It's an incredible experience, and it looks amazing on a college application.

TJ: How was your experience running last year?

Crystal: It was stressful at first, but once I started writing my speech and putting it into words, I realized how easy it was. You just have to take all that emotion of how bad you want it and use it to put together the best presentation you can.

TJ: Thank you so much for even responding. I can't imagine how busy you probably are. I always felt embarrassed to ask, I don't wanna sound desperate.

Crystal: No, you're fine! It's the end of my senior year; I'm rarely busy. I actually respect you wanting my advice and being vocal about it, I know that's a nerve-wracking thing to do.

Crystal: And let me take the opportunity to say thank you for all the stuff you drew for the bulletin board, it all looked so good.

TJ: Thank you so much, that means a lot! I always loved the work you made that the art teacher would leave on display in his room. Where are you going for college?

Crystal: Aw, thank you! I actually just got accepted to an art and design school in the city.

TJ: You're welcome! And that's awesome!

Crystal: Thank you!
Crystal: If it's okay for me to ask, what pronouns do you go by?

TJ: I've always gone by he/him, but I just started going by she/her.
TJ: After what you did on Trans Visibility Day, it's been a lot easier being myself in school, and I've even been able to come out at home. You've changed my life for the better, and you're such an inspiration. Thank you so much.

Crystal: That means so much to hear. I'm so happy to hear that! Being visibly trans is a battle, but it's not impossible. The way to win that battle is to hold your head high, stay proud, and always remember your worth and individuality, not just as a trans person but as a person.

TJ: It's amazing to get to talk to you about this. What is it that gave you all that confidence to do what you do? You're seriously braver than anyone else that's walked those halls.

Crystal: Thank you so much for saying that. It's lovely to hear, but the truth is I don't hear it often, and truthfully, for a long time people made me feel the exact opposite. No matter how confident or proud of myself, I was, it didn't matter because of all the negative things I heard to my face and from behind my back. But eventually, I met someone who told me to take advantage of my disadvantages, and I learned how to use what people told me was awful about myself to raise awareness and spread the message of equality. This island may be closed minded and conservative, but we have to remember there is a whole world past it filled with loving and accepting people.

TJ: Thank you for being such an inspiration.

Crystal: Thank you for doing the same for me.

I remember going to school for the first time. I remember my first teacher from Pre K. I remember I would draw pictures for her. I remember how she said she loved every single one. I remember starting to have a hard time getting along with the other kids. I sometimes remember when my imagination was too much for everyone else. I remember the last day of school that year when we celebrated my birthday. I remember my family got to come. I remember all the pictures my mom took. I remember this is when I fell in love with being the center of attention. I remember how amazing of a day that was.

I remember when things started getting harder in Kindergarten. I remember how mean my kindergarten teacher was. I remember having to tell my class I wanted to grow up to be a doctor because a prince wasn't an acceptable answer. I remember my teacher calling me weird. I remember her being right. I remember her telling me I was never gonna make it to 1ˢᵗ grade. I remember making it to 1ˢᵗ grade.

I remember how much I loved 2ⁿᵈ grade. I remember being praised for my creativity for once. I remember getting to share my writing in writers workshop to the whole class and have fun with storytelling my way. I remember falling in love with performing this year. I remember this was the year I got to be in my first school play. I remember this is how I fell in love with theater.

Confessions of a Teenage Playwright

I've always had a serious passion for creating and telling stories because of all the books and movies I fell in love with at an early age. I was obsessed with the concept of fantastical happenings and happy endings invented by stories of fantasy. I didn't have the brightest or happiest upbringing; most of my happiness came from any means of storytelling. I was inspired by the stories I loved as a kid to create my own stories and concepts. When I grew up and saw that these stories that I loved all started as an idea in someone's head, I realized I had that power in me to bring my own ideas to life. From a young age, I started making my own books out of computer paper, a pen, a stapler, and a dream. I started by writing my own versions of fairy tales because my happiest place as a little kid was in the fairy tale and fantasy sections of the library. I truly believed I would be a published author by the time I turned 16. But a lot of other passions I had got in the way of where I wanted my life to go. Still, I noticed writing kept coming back.

I wrote for the school newspaper. I wrote and performed a monologue for the annual drama club show. I wrote essays that became best in the class; I won a $2,000 scholarship for my writing. Right after high school, my original play was selected for an off-Broadway theater festival, and I was able to bring my character, Crystal, to life on stage in her blue masquerade ball gown. But it's hard to take on such a big role at such a young age. I wore the hats of director, writer, producer, and lead actor, when all I had done before that point was set and costume design. But at such a young age, all I cared about was the experience and having a good time. The first run of my play I'm proud of, no matter what standards anyone else held, I know I did my best, which was all I could do. The part that hurt was performing alongside other young actors who fooled me with friendship to get their spot on stage and jumpstart their own careers. Some wonderful friendships came from the experience, but by others, I felt used.

After the first run ended, I hit a low point in life. I went from my biggest pride to a depressed, struggling first-year college student. I clung onto the script, hopeful it could get picked up again. I went into the following year optimistic, and I was lucky enough to be given another stage in an LGBTQ theater workshop. This time I worked with a more experienced editor and director, and older, more experienced actors. I again got to bring Crystal to life, but I'd come to regret this run of my show, as the person I had trusted to direct was not one to be trusted with my script, or with me at all. His intentions went past, wanting to put my story on stage. That was the last time I performed that version of the script. That same director pushed me to submit my personal script to bigger, grander stages, only to face rejection. But I knew if I were to showcase this story again, I had to remaster it my own way.

I miraculously became one of the youngest known performed playwrights by what feels like a miracle, or an accident. This will forever be an amazing memory and accomplishment that has helped me grow and learn more about myself and where I want to go. But

I don't want to let one big accomplishment from this early, confusing stage of my life define the rest of it. I have too many other dreams.

HOW MY PLAY ENDED

Act 2 Scene 9: Outside Victory Ballroom

(Lights; Tom is outside, alone, waiting for Maria and Crystal. Anna enters.)

Anna: Hey, who are you waiting for?

Tom: My cousin.

Anna: Maria? Is she with Crystal?

Tom: Don't worry about it.

Anna: I'm surprised you're civil with Crystal despite everything

Tom: Since you lied to her and tried to ruin our friendship. What'd you even tell her to get her to believe you?

Anna: (Smirking) I showed her a screenshot of something Drew said about her a while ago

Tom: You are so twisted.

Anna: I'm only trying to help you.

Tom: Oh, please. You try to convince her that all boys are heartbreakers. You're only doing that to her because you're the insecure one, so you're trying to make Crystal feel the same way. Well, I'm going to convince her that not all guys are like that.

Anna: What are you talking about? (Pause) Oh my god, you have feelings for her? (Overhears Crystal and Maria getting close) Well, (Moving in on Tom) I can help you get over her.

Tom: What are you doing?

Anna: Trying to take your mind off her. (She tries to kiss Tom.)

Tom: I don't want your help

(Tom pushes Anna away. Anna grabs Tom and kisses him, just as Crystal enters)

Crystal: Tom… (Sees them kissing and her jaw drops.)

(They stop kissing. Crystal runs off.)

Tom: No, wait! (He runs after her.)

Act 2 Scene 10: Victory Ballroom

(Lights go on, Crystal's hiding as Tom runs in)

Tom: Crystal! I know you're here (Pause.) Come on, answer me. (Another pause.)

(Crystal hesitantly comes out.)

Tom: Anna force kissed me. That wasn't a real kiss.

Crystal: (Trying to get passed Tom) Why should I believe you?

Tom: (Steps in front of Crystal every time she tries to move) I get it, you've been heartbroken, you have trust issues, but please believe that I don't want to hurt you.

Crystal: You really think you know me so well, don't you?

Tom: Maybe I don't know you all that much, but through and through, I trust you.

Crystal: This is really that important to you?

Tom: There's something that I should admit to you…

Crystal: What is it?

Tom: In life, there are people we meet that we feel we have a connection with, like the kind of magic love you read about in stories.

Crystal: Get to the point!

Tom: Crystal, I feel like I'm in love with you.

226

(Crystal starts pinching herself.)

Tom: What are you doing?

Crystal: Trying to wake me up. This is obviously a dream.

Tom: (Grabbing Crystal's hands and stops her, then let's go) Is it true that you like me too?

Crystal: Yes. But what do you see in me?

Tom: You're such a brave, strong, and amazingly beautiful person.

Crystal: You really feel that way about me?

Tom: I don't feel it. I know it.

Crystal: You know what I like about you? You're smart, handsome, and kind. At first, I thought you were super nice to me, but then I saw how gracious you are to everyone around you. You're the first guy to be my true friend and be there for me and listen if I need to talk. It sucks there aren't that many people out there like you.

Tom: You know what's even worse? That there aren't as many people out there like you.

(They kiss. The scene ends; lights go off)

Who wrote this shit?

ANNA'S PHONE

May 21st

5:59 PM

Drew: Hey.

Anna: Hey.
Anna: What's up?

Drew: Not much, just wanted to know how you're doing.

Anna: Honestly, I'm doing really well. I feel better than I have in a long time.

Drew: That's so good to hear.

Anna: Not to act like I'm not happy to hear from you, but why hit me up out of nowhere?

Drew: I can't help but feel guilty about something.

Anna: And that would be?

Drew: Telling Shay about what happened with you and Crystal.
Drew: I thought she could be trusted because she was your friend.

228

Anna: If she's asking you something about someone else it's not because she cares, it's because she wants something new to gossip about. Just like the rest of them.

Drew: Are you mad at me?

Anna: Honestly, why should I be? What they say, and think doesn't mean anything to me anymore. That school isn't for me; it never was.

Drew: Thanks, but a part of me does wish we never had that falling out.

Anna: But Drew, why? After everything, I've done, especially to you? I treated you horribly, and I eventually made you do something that I was too scared to do. I have been doing better, but that's still with me every day. I'm sorry, and I don't deserve your forgiveness.

Drew: But I do forgive you.

Anna: You really are such a good guy. It's so hard to be okay with myself knowing how bad I treated you. You didn't deserve that.

Drew: All we can do is move past it.
Drew: Is there anything else you regret?

Anna: I was excited about prom. But why would I spend all that money just to be around a ton of people that don't respect me?

Anna: But at the same time, it's every girl's dream, as much as my dreams have changed, it still would've been nice to see that dream come true.

Drew: If it is something you want to do, I'd love to take you as my date.

Anna: Yes.

Anna: Yes.

Anna: Oh my god, YES!

Anna: Is it too late? Can we still make that happen?

Drew: Yeah, my table has an extra seat. Besides, we were planning on going to prom together all throughout last year, weren't we?

Anna: Drew, this means so much to me, thank you so much!

Anna: Wanna hang out tomorrow? We can figure out what we're wearing, start planning everything out.

Drew: Yeah, sounds good. I'll text you tomorrow!

Anna: Awesome, can't wait!

CRYSTAL'S PHONE

June 10th

11:52 AM

Suzy: Happy Prom Day, everyone!!

Gus: Guys, I'm bugging. I forgot to make an appointment to get my nails done. Prom. Is. RUINED!

Luke: You're still the perfect prom date with or without fake nails <3

Gus: Ugh, I have the best boyfriend, I love you <3

Luke: I'm your boyfriend?

Gus: You sure are.

Crystal: Maria, what time am I meeting you at the salon??

Maria: An hour. Then we'll go to my house to get ready for pre-prom?

Crystal: Yeah, Tracy said she'll bring all my stuff to your house.
Crystal: Suzy, are you coming with us?

Suzy: I was never asked to, but I will if you want.

231

Crystal: Oh, I kinda just assumed, aren't you and Maria going as dates?

Suzy: No, I don't have a date.

Crystal: Wait, I'm confused. Maria, you said you had a date.

Maria: I do...
Maria: It's Tom.

Gus: Shook

Maria: Look, he's practically my family, and I don't want him to miss his senior prom. So, that's why Suzy and I aren't going together.

Suzy: And I'm fine with that!

Maria: It's been over a year. All that drama should be a thing of the past. We should be coming together now to celebrate what we've been through and that we got through it.

Crystal: You're totally right. Can't wait for tonight <3

June 10th

8:25 PM

Anna: Hey, where are you?

Crystal: Maria and I ran to the bathroom. Why what's up?

Anna: I'm on the balcony, come take a picture with me!

Crystal: You don't think Mom and Dad took enough at pre-prom?

Anna: This is prom, there can never be enough pictures.

Crystal: True, I'll be right out.

Anna: Drew and I can't get over your dress, I can't believe you made that. You need to show me how to sew.

Crystal: Thank you! And OMG, I'd love that!

Anna: If it's okay to ask, how are you and Tom getting along?

Crystal: We're fine, we're getting along, and that's all I need. He's mostly been with Maria throughout the night. Seeing him brings back memories, but I'm not bothered.

Anna: I saw the way you looked at him. And I can see the way he looks at you. If there are hidden feelings, don't deny them. You'll only regret it.
Anna: Now, stop texting me and get out here.

Crystal: I'll be right out.

Anna: Let's go dance after the pics??

Crystal: Oh of course <3

June 10th

9:45 PM

Gus: So, like...
Gus: You guys saw what I saw, right?

Luke: Yep.

Maria: Oh yeah

Suzy: Wait, I'm so confused, what happened?

Gus: Crystal and Tom started dancing with each other, just like their slow dance at the ball.

Suzy: OMG!
Suzy: Maria, your date!

Maria: Oh, I'm not mad. I'm happy for them.

Suzy: Oh, I know, but if Crystal's dancing with him, why aren't we dancing together?

Maria: You're so right!

Gus: How did they even end up dancing together?

Maria: Why question it? Just be happy for them.

Luke: Almost everyone left the dance floor and stared at them like they were an exhibit in a museum.

Gus: Yet the two of them are still dancing, looking beautiful and happy as ever, Crystal's skirt flowing like a cloud whenever he spins her. It's like they're in their own world.

Luke: Let's go dance with them!

June 11th

12:00 AM

Crystal: Guys, where's my shoe?

Gus: What are you talking about?

Crystal: After Tom and I went our separate ways, I took my heels off and left them under the table, but one of them is gone.

Luke: You're gonna have to just leave it, the limo's coming to pick us up any minute.

Crystal: I don't wanna just leave my shoe.

Luke: I know it sucks, but the limos not gonna wait for us and we can't leave you behind.

Crystal: Alright, I'll be right out.

June 11th

8:18 AM

Tom: Good morning!

Crystal: What's up? Why weren't you in the limo with
Maria last night?

Tom: I actually ended up going with some of my
friends. Maria was fine with it. She was happy that I was
getting to see my old friends again.
Tom: I felt bad for leaving after our dance, but
truthfully, I didn't know if you wanted me around.

Crystal: After the dance, we had you really believe
that?

Tom: You did leave me on read when I tried to
congratulate you on your GSA presidency.

Crystal: And you left me read all throughout summer
when I tried to talk to you.

Tom: And you just flat out stopped talking to me the
Monday after the ball when all those rumors were going
around, and you relished in every moment while I was
left in the mud.

Crystal: To be fair, I thought you were trying to use
me.

Tom: Do you still think that?

Crystal: After last night, no. Getting to see to you again as if nothing had happened reminded me of all the things that first made me like you: your kindness, your smile, just your overall charm. When the slow song came on, and you took my hand, I felt like we were the only ones there.

Tom: We were at one point.

Crystal: But when everyone joined us on the dance floor, after Gus, Luke, Maria, Suzy, Anna, and Drew slowly joined us. It felt like our connection at that moment unified everyone back together.

Tom: You really thought it was that magical?

Crystal: Yeah.

Tom: Good, I hoped it wasn't just me.
Tom: Anyways, I'm an idiot for not taking the limo with you guys because I have something to give you.

Crystal: What?

Tom: Your shoe.

Crystal: Tom, are you serious?! I almost lost my mind when I couldn't find my shoe, why did you take it?

Tom: I didn't just take it, there were some kids trying to mess with your stuff. They took your shoe, so I told them off and took it back.

Crystal: So why didn't you either put it back or give it to me?

Tom: I figured I had an excuse to see you again.

Crystal: You're a freak.

Tom: You out of all people would call someone that?

Crystal: Don't go there.

Tom: What were you hoping we would dance with each other and share a magical night, and then you could drop me, just like you did last time?

Crystal: I'm about 2 seconds away from blocking your number.

Tom: Why? After everything we went through, every conversation, heart to heart, bus ride, our dances, our kiss. It hurt me so bad that you walked those halls proud of yourself for dancing with someone who loved you, then running away from them, then ghosting them. I get I wasn't an angel but stop acting like an entitled brat just because you're different! It doesn't give you any right to treat me the way that you did.

Crystal: You're right. I'm sorry. You didn't deserve that.

Tom: It's like there were no walls between us then after Drew started talking on the loudspeaker, every wall just went right back up, just like from the day we first met. Why?

Crystal: I was embarrassed. I didn't know what you were really thinking, and I was scared of it. So I avoided it. Maybe I was scared of getting hurt; maybe I was scared of hurting you. When I realized what I had to focus on to work on myself, I only committed to that, and I felt you were distracting me. I'm sorry if that sounds mean but look what happened when I committed to accomplishing my goals.

Tom: But I could've been by your side throughout all of that. We let high school drama ruin this for both of us.

Crystal: I know. It's one of my biggest regrets. It's the one goal I never got to achieve. But that's all in the past. I wanna move on from it.

Tom: Where do we go from here?

Crystal: Why don't we meet up and talk this out in person? This texting thing is so stupid.

Tom: We can go on a walk.

Crystal: I'd like that.

Crystal: Please bring my shoe.

Tom: I will.

Crystal: Thank you.

I'm going to explain my situation as simply as I can. I'm a shoe. I'm a *pink, sparkling, high heeled* shoe, adorned with *bows* and a detailed pattern of *flowers* and *butterflies*. I'm **"girly."** I'm **hyper-feminine**. I'm **flamboyant**. I'm a **girl's** shoe. But a big mistake was made. I live in a box for a **boy's** sneaker. A *blue, boring* box, for a *boy's* shoe. Imagine the feeling of opening the box & finding the exact opposite inside. The *confusion*. The *disappointment*. Just an overall feeling of not knowing what to do. Or at least that's what I've experienced.

When people see my box first, they're expecting one thing. When they see the shoe I am **inside;** *I don't make sense to them*. But ***I like myself for the shoe that I am***. I like being **over the top**. I like being *noticed*. I like being the ***center of attention***. But sometimes I like the subtlety and the security of my box. So, I embrace both. *I use my disadvantage to my advantage*, even if it confuses those around me.

When I face rejection, I'm left with my dreams and my aspirations.

Maybe I'll belong to a model and get to walk on a runway or red carpet.

Maybe I'll belong to a drag queen and get to celebrate myself through art.

There's no reason to ever feel broken or alone in this world of expectations and harsh opinions. After all, this mistake is made all the time. *There are plenty of high heeled, dazzling women's shoes in shoe boxes for men's sneakers or boots, same as there are plenty of men's shoes living in shoe boxes for women's shoes.* No matter what the box, **all those shoes, including me, are unique and fulfill their purpose.**

Dear Crystal,

You and I have a similar mindset when it comes to high school. It sucks. I know how difficult it is when you feel like your connection to everyone around you is broken. I know that awful feeling of being looked down upon by those around you, from faculty members who roll their eyes at the sight of you, or the students who overshadow your accomplishments only because they are what's considered normal. Accomplishments such as being president of a Gay-Straight Alliance, and helping design costumes for a school play, only for them to be invalidated not just by students, but teachers. Unfortunately, no matter what you accomplish, those around you will make it out as if you're not as worthy as they are, just because you're different.

I know how scary it is to face backlash on a daily basis. I know what it's like hearing all those threats and insults being whispered about you or screamed at you, but still having to keep a straight face. I know how naked you feel when everyone's staring at you when you're just trying to mind your own business. And I know how

245

frustrating it is to always have that question, "Why?" But the best answer you can get is that it's just High School, and it will be over before you know it. There's not much you can learn from a facility that favors popularity over kindness. The opinions of others does not take away any real friend you made, any good memory you have, any teacher who encouraged you, or any of your stellar accomplishments. We ran a GSA, designed costumes for a play, hung up a pride flag, won a scholarship, and those kids who made fun of you are now treasuring a senior t-shirt designed by you.

In the darkest moments, remember what you do this for. For every kid who feels outcast and rejected. Your strength and bravery, and everything you've achieved reminds me of why it was all worth it. Remember, this is not just your story. This story of triumph is universal. People across the globe are experiencing this story, just their own version of it. And some don't make it to their happy ending. Now that you did use your voice and your story to spread the message now that you have the opportunity.

Always remember, *Pride is Power.*

Sincerely,
The Most Popular Freak in School

72418406R00149